A Time to Grow

BETHANY HOUSE PUBLISHERS

The Novels of George MacDonald Edited for Today's Reader

Edited Title	Original Title
The Fisherman's Lady	*Malcolm*
The Marquis' Secret	*The Marquis of Lossie*
The Baronet's Song	*Sir Gibbie*
The Shepherd's Castle	*Donal Grant*
The Tutor's First Love	*David Elginbrod*
The Musician's Quest	*Robert Falconer*
The Maiden's Bequest	*Alec Forbes*
The Curate's Awakening	*Thomas Wingfold*
The Lady's Confession	*Paul Faber*
The Baron's Apprenticeship	*There and Back*
The Highlander's Last Song	*What's Mine's Mine*
The Gentlewoman's Choice	*Weighed and Wanting*
The Laird's Inheritance	*Warlock O'Glenwarlock*
The Minister's Restoration	*Salted with Fire*
A Daughter's Devotion	*Mary Marston*
The Peasant Girl's Dream	*Heather and Snow*
The Landlady's Master	*The Elect Lady*
The Poet's Homecoming	*Home Again*

MacDonald Classics Edited for Young Readers
Wee Sir Gibbie of the Highlands
Alec Forbes and His Friend Annie
At the Back of the North Wind

George MacDonald: Scotland's Beloved Storyteller
by Michael Phillips
Discovering the Character of God by George MacDonald
Knowing the Heart of God by George MacDonald

GEORGE MACDONALD CLASSIC DEVOTIONALS

A TIME TO GROW

Inspiring Devotional Selections from the writings of

George MacDonald

Compiled and Edited by
Michael R. Phillips

BETHANY HOUSE PUBLISHERS
Minneapolis, Minnesota 55438

Published by Bethany House Publishers
A Ministry of Bethany Fellowship, Inc.
6820 Auto Club Road, Minneapolis, Minnesota 55438

Printed in the United States of America

Library of Congress Cataloging-in-Publication Data

MacDonald, George, 1824–1905.
    George MacDonald classic devotionals / George MacDonald :
compiled and edited by Michael R. Phillips.
      p. cm.
    Selections from the novels, sermons, and poetry in a
devotional format.
    Contents: [1] A time to grow
    ISBN 1-55661-202-8 (v. 1)
    1. Devotional literature. English.   I. Phillips, Michael R.,
1946–   .   II. Title.   III. Title: Classic devotionals.
BV4832. M17   1991
242—dc20   91-10427
                                         CIP

CONTENTS

INTRODUCTION

Scottish novelist and poet George MacDonald (1824–1905) was a writer of such depth and diversity that his books often seem daunting at first glance. If his complex thoughts and lofty spiritual ideas are not enough to overwhelm some, the Scottish dialect in many of his novels can intimidate the most adventurous of readers. Add to this the fact that most of MacDonald's books are over 400 pages in length—sometimes even five, six, or seven hundred in their original editions—and it is not difficult to understand why his readership in the past has been loyal but rather small.

I am one of those few loyal readers, and years ago was born in my heart the vision of reintroducing Mac-Donald to today's readers. I was pleased to find a publisher who shared this vision, and Bethany House Publishers and I teamed up to select, edit, and publish eighteen of his novels to date. The number of books sold since the first one, *The Fisherman's Lady*, was published in 1982 has been gratifying, and even more so are the personal responses from new MacDonald fans.

For years my good friends at Bethany have talked about MacDonald devotional books comprised of brief passages from some of his novels. Our hope is to offer concise selections that capture some of the incidents, relationships, conversations, and observations from MacDonald's stories that highlight his insights and perspectives. For readers familiar with his books, such passages in a devotional format can serve as rewarding reminders of past reading experiences as well as become vehicles for personal encounters with God. For those still unfamiliar with MacDonald, these devotional excerpts offer an introductory exposure to George Mac-

Donald's deep spiritual insight through the characters and events in his novels. Appropriate poetry pieces and parallel selections from his sermons add further insight into MacDonald's breadth of spiritual understanding.

We have built this series of devotional compilations on a seasonal theme, since the yearly changes of nature played such a prominent role in MacDonald's own life and in his stories. *A Time to Grow* centers on a summer theme, both literally and figuratively. The publisher and I invite you to let these devotional readings make a time for growth in your own life.

Mike Phillips
February, 1991

TEARS OF WINTER/ WINDS OF SUMMER

IT WAS NOT ALL FINE WEATHER UP THERE among the mountains in the beginning of summer. In the first week of June even, there was sleet and snow in the wind—the tears of the vanquished Winter, as he fled across the sea from Norway or Iceland. Then would Donal's heart be sore for Gibbie, when he saw his poor rags blown about like streamers in the wind.

Donal had neither greatcoat, plaid, nor umbrella wherewith to shield Gibbie's raggedness. Once in great pity he pulled off his jacket and threw it on Gibbie's shoulders. But the shout of laughter that burst from the boy as he flung the jacket from him and rushed away into the middle of the feeding herd, a shout that came from no rudeness but from the very depths of delight stirred by the loving-kindness of the act, startled Donal out of his pity into brief anger.

But Gibbie dived under the belly of a favorite cow and, peering out sideways from under her while the cow went on undisturbed, showed such an innocent countenance of merriment that the pride of Donal's hurt melted away and his laughter echoed Gibbie's.

The Baronet's Song, p. 59

How excellent is thy lovingkindness, O God!
therefore the children of men put their trust
under the shadow of thy wings.
Psalm 36:7

THE GLORY OF A COUNTRY SUMMER

AFTER SCHOOL WAS OUT, WHAT A DELIGHT-ful walk of three miles the boys had to Mr. Lammie's farm—over hill and dale and moor and farm.

That first summer walk was to Robert something to remember in after years with nothing short of ecstasy. The westering sun threw long shadows before them as they trudged away eastward, lightly laden with the books they needed for tomorrow's lessons. Once beyond the immediate environs of the town and the various place of land occupied by its inhabitants, they crossed a small river and entered a region of little hills, some covered with trees, others cultivated, and some bearing only heather, now nursing in secret its purple flame for the outburst of autumn.

The road wound between, now swampy and worn into deep ruts, now sandy and broken with large stones. Here and there green fields, fenced with stones over-grown with moss, would stretch away on both sides, sprinkled with busily feeding cattle.

They passed through an occasional farmstead, per-fumed with the breath of cows and the odor of burning peat. The scent of the oaks and larches would steal from the hills, or the wind would waft the odor of the white clover to Robert's nostrils, and he would turn aside to pull his grandmother a handful.

Then they climbed a high ridge, on the top of which spread a moorland, dreary and desolate. This crossed, they descended between young plantations of firs and rowan trees and birches till they reached a warm house on the side of the slope, with farm buildings and ricks

of corn and hay all about it, the front overgrown with roses and honeysuckle.

From the open kitchen door came the smell of something good. But beyond all was the welcome of Miss Lammie, whose small, pudgy hand closed upon his like a very love pudding to warm his heart.

What a wonderful time were those next few days at Bodyfauld. To a boy like Robert, the daily changes from country to town with the bright morning, from town to country with the sober evening, were a source of boundless delight. Instead of houses he saw the horizon; instead of streets or walled gardens he roamed over the fields, bathed in sunlight and wind.

Here it was especially good to get up before the sun, for then he could see the sun get up. And of all things, those evening shadows, lengthening out over the grassy wildernesses, were a deepening marvel.

The Musician's Quest, pp. 85–86

The Lord's . . . compassions fail not. They are new every morning: great is thy faithfulness.
Lamentations 3:22–23

The truth of the sky is what it makes us feel of the God that sent it out to our eyes. . . . In its discovered laws, light seems to me to be such because God is such. Its so-called laws are the waving of his garments, waving so because he is thinking and loving and walking inside them.

Discovering the Character of God, p. 59;
Unspoken Sermons, Third Series—"The Truth"

THE MYSTERY OF THE WOOD

IT WAS NOW EARLY SUMMER, AND ALL THE trees had put on their fresh leaves. In the morning the sun shone so clear upon them that, to the eyes of one standing beneath, the light seemed to dissolve them away to the most ethereal forms. Margaret continued to haunt the wood nearly every morning.

Margaret's mental interests and facilities deepened noticeably. She began to read Wordsworth and others, and found herself introduced to nature in altogether new aspects which had hitherto been unknown to her. Not only was the fir wood now dearer to her than before, but its mystery seemed more sacred. And the purple hillside grew as dear as the wood, and her morning walks took her farther and farther from the cottage. Now taller and more graceful, the lasting quiet of her face began slowly to blossom into a constant expression of loveliness.

The Tutor's First Love, p. 24

The heavens declare the glory of God; and the firmament sheweth his handywork.
Psalm 19:1

I believe that every fact in nature is a revelation of God. . . . From the moment when first we come into contact with the world, it is to us a revelation of God, his things seen, by which we come to know the things unseen.   *Discovering the Character of God, p. 59;*
Unspoken Sermons, Third Series—"The Truth"

AWAKE TO JOY

THE SEASON WENT ON, AND THE WORLD, like a great flower afloat in space, kept opening its thousandfold blossoms. Hail and sleet were things lost in the distance of the year—storming away in some far-off region of the north, unknown to the summer generation.

The butterflies, with wings looking as if all the flower painters of fairyland had wiped their brushes upon them in freakful yet artistic sport, came forth in the freedom of their wills and the faithful ignorance of their minds. The birds, the poets of the animal creation, awoke to utter their own joy and awake a similar joy in others of God's children. *The Maiden's Bequest, pp. 121–122*

*Nevertheless he left not himself without
witness, in that he did good, and gave us rain
from heaven, and fruitful seasons, filling our
hearts with food and gladness.*
Acts 14:17

The truth of a thing, then, is the blossom of it, the thing it is made for, the topmost stone set on with rejoicing. Truth in a man's imagination is the power to recognize this truth of a thing. And wherever, in anything that God has made, in the glory of it, be it sky or flower or human face, we see the glory of God, there a true imagination is beholding a truth of God. *Discovering the Character of God, p. 66;*
Unspoken Sermons, Third Series—"The Truth"

THE BUDDING PHILOSOPHY OF YOUTH

THE BOY SAT ON A BIG STONE, WHICH ONCE must have had something to do with the house itself or its defenses, but which he had never known as anything except a seat for him to sit upon. He was already more than a budding philosopher, though he could not yet have put into recognizable shape the thought that was now passing through his mind.

In brief it was this: he was thinking about how glad the bees would be when their crop of heather was ripe; then he thought how they preferred the heather to the flowers; then, that the one must taste the nicer to them than the other. This last thought awoke the question whether their taste of sweet was the same as his. If it was, he thought to himself, then there was something in the makeup of the bee that was the same with the makeup of the boy. And if that was true, then perhaps someday a boy might, if he wanted, try out the taste of being a bee for a little while.

To look at the boy as he sat there, nobody would have thought he was doing anything but basking in the sun. The scents of the flowers all about his feet came and went on the eddies of the air, while the windy noises of the insects, the watery noises of the pigeons, the noises from the poultry yard, and the song of the mountain river all visited his brain as well through the portal of his ears. But at the moment the boy seemed lost in the mere fundamental satisfaction of existence.

Broad summer was indeed on the earth and the whole land was for a time bathed in sunlight. Yet although the country was his native land, and he loved it with the love of his country's poets, the consciousness of the boy could not break free from a certain strange kind of trouble—connected with, if not resulting from the landscape before him. He was a Celt through many of his ancestors, and his mother in particular, and his soul was thus full of undefined emotion and an ever-recurring impulse to break out in song.

The Laird's Inheritance, p. 19

*The Lord is my strength and my shield; my
heart trusted in him, and I am helped:
therefore my heart greatly rejoiceth; and with
my song will I praise him.*
Psalm 28:7

When a man bows obediently down before a Power that can account for him, as a child whom his father is leading by the hand to the heights of happy-making truth—then is that man bursting into his flower. Then the truth of his being, his real nature, begins to show itself. Then is his nature coming into harmony with itself.

In obeying the will that is the cause of his being, he begins to stand on the apex of his being.

Discovering the Character of God, pp. 67–68;
Unspoken Sermons, Third Series—"The Truth"

THE GLADNESS OF SUMMER

IN THE MIDDLE OF THE SUMMER MR. CUPPLES made his appearance and was warmly welcomed. He had at length completed the catalogue of the library, had got the books arranged to his satisfaction, and was a brimful of enjoyment.

He ran about the fields like a child; gathered bunches of white clover; made a great kite and bought an unmeasurable length of string, with which he flew it the first day the wind was worthy of the honor. He got out Alec's boat and capsized himself in the Glamour—fortunately, in shallow water; was run away with by one of the plow horses in the attempt to ride him to the water, and was laughed at and loved by everybody about Howglen.

The Maiden's Bequest, p. 267

The pastures are clothed with flocks; the
valleys also are covered over with corn; they
shout for joy, they also sing.
Psalm 65:13

The heavens and the earth are around us that it may be possible for us to speak of the unseen by the seen, for the outermost husk of creation has correspondence with the deepest things of the Creator.

He is not a God that hides himself, but a God who made all that he might reveal himself.

Knowing the Heart of God, p. 96;
Unspoken Sermons, Third Series—"The Knowing of the Son"

WHO BUT GOD COULD INVENT ROSES?

IT REMAINED A QUESTION AS TO WHETHER or not there was a supreme being putting forth claims of obedience. And though Paul Faber considered such imaginary, it remained for him an uncomfortable sort of phantom to have brooding above him, continually coming between him and the freedom of an otherwise empty universe.

To the human soul as I have learned to know it, an empty universe would be as an exhausted airbag to the lungs that thirst for air. But Faber liked the idea: how he would have liked the *reality* remains another thing. I suspect that even what we call damnation can never exist; for even the damned live by God's life.

The summer at length reigned lordly in the land. The roses were in bloom, from the black purple to the warm white. Ah, those roses! He must indeed be a God who invented the roses. They sank into the red hearts of men and women, caused old men to sigh, young men to long, and women to weep with strange ecstatic sadness.   *The Lady's Confession, pp. 102–103*

*Honour and majesty are before him: strength
and beauty are in his sanctuary.
Psalm 96:6*

Nature Embodies the Character of God

MARY HAD ALWAYS BEEN RATHER A PRIVATE person, and so was little known even among the religious associates of her father. There are few of the so-called religious who seem able to trust either God or their neighbor in matters that concern these two and no other. Nor had she had opportunity of making acquaintance with any who believed and lived like her father in any of the other churches of the town. But she had her Bible, and when that troubled her, as it did sometimes, she had God himself to cry to for such wisdom as she could receive. And one of the things she learned was that nowhere in the Bible was she called on to believe in the Bible, but in the living God in whom is no darkness, and who alone can give light to understand his own intent. All her troubles she carried to him.

It was not always the solitude of her room that Mary sought to get out of the wind of the world. Her love of nature had been growing stronger after her father's death.

If the world is God's, every true man and woman ought to feel at home in it. Something is wrong if the calm of the summer night does not sink into the heart, for it embodies the peace of God. Something is wrong in the man to whom the sunrise is not a divine glory, for therein are embodied the truth, the simplicity, and the might of the Maker.

When all is true in us, we shall feel the visible presence of God's watchful eye and loving hand. For the

things that he works are their signs and symbols, their clothing fact. In the gentle meeting of earth and sky, in the witnessing colors of the west, in the wind that so gently visited her cheek in the great burst of a new morning, Mary saw the sordid affairs of Mammon, to whose worship the shop seemed to become more and more of a temple, sink to the bottom of things, as the mud, which, during the day the feet of the drinking cattle have stirred, sinks in the silent night to the bottom of the clear pool. And she saw that the sordid is all in the soul, and not in the shop. The service of Christ is help. The service of Mammon is greed. *A Daughter's Devotion, pp. 121–122*

No man can serve two masters: for either he will hate the one, and love the other; or else he will hold to the one, and despise the other. Ye cannot serve God and mammon.

Matthew 6:24

The whole system of divine education regarding the relation of man to man has for its end that a man should love his neighbor as himself.

This is, however, so far from being universally accepted as truth, that the greater number even of those calling themselves Christians believe, on the contrary, that the paramount obligation of life is to take care of one's self at much risk of forgetting one's neighbor. *Knowing the Heart of God, p. 324;*

Unspoken Sermons, First Series—"Love Thy Neighbor"

THE SWEET MUSIC OF SUMMER

ONE EVENING, TOWARD THE END OF JULY, when the summer is at its peak and makes the world feel as if there had never been and never ought to be anything but summer, Hester was sitting under a fir tree, pine odors filling the air around her, as if they, too, stole out with the things of the night when the sun was gone. The sweet melancholy of the hour moved her spirit. So close was her heart to nature that when alone with it, she seldom longed for her piano. She *had* the music and did not need to hear it.   *The Gentlewoman's Choice, p. 88*

Sing, O ye heavens; for the Lord hath done
it: shout, ye lower parts of the earth: break
forth into singing, ye mountains, O forest,
and every tree therein: for the Lord hath
redeemed Jacob, and glorified himself in Israel.
Isaiah 44:23

When a man is true, he is right with himself, because right with him from whom he came. To be right with God is to be right with the universe; one with the power, the love, the will of the mighty Father, the cherisher of joy, the Lord of laughter, whose are all glories, all hopes, who loves everything, and hates nothing but selfishness, which he will not have in his kingdom.

Discovering the Character of God, p. 69;
Unspoken Sermons, Third Series—"The Truth"

22

The Lifting of the Heart with a Sense of Presence

IT WAS NOW MIDSUMMER, AND FRANCIS Gordon was well, though looking thin and rather delicate. Kirsty and he had walked together to the top of the Horn, and there sat in the heart of old memories.

The sun was clouded above. The boggy basin lay dark below, with its rim of heathery hills not yet in bloom, and its bottom of peaty marsh, green and black, with here and there a shining spot. The growing crops of the far-off farms on the other side but little affected the general impression the view gave of a waste world.

Yet the wide expanse of heaven and earth lifted Kirsty's heart with an indescribable sense of presence, purpose, and promise. For was it not the country on which, fresh from God, she first opened the eyes of this life, the visible region in which all her efforts had gone forth, in which all the food of her growth had been gathered, in which all her joys had come to her, in which all her loves had their scope, the place whence by and by she would go away to find her brother with the bonny man!

Francis looked without heeding, saw without seeing. His heart was not uplifted.   *The Peasant Girl's Dream, p. 188*

Let the heaven and earth praise him, the seas,
and every thing that moveth therein.
Psalm 69:34

RADIANT WITH EXPECTATION

AS HELEN LOOKED OUT ON THE FRESH reviving of nature's universal law of birth, she was conscious that her own life, her own self, had risen from the dead, had been newborn also. She did not have to look back far to the time when all was dull and dead in her own being. Then came the earthquake, and the storm, and the fire, and after them the still small voice breathing new life and hope and strength. Now her whole world was radiant with expectation.

It was through her husband that the change had come, but he was not the rock on which she built. For his sake she could willingly go to hell—even cease to exist; but there was one whom she loved more than he— the one whose love had sent forth her husband and herself to love one another; whose heart was the nest of their birth, the cradle of their growth, the rest of their being. In him, the perfect love, she hoped for a perfect love toward her husband, and a perfect nature in herself.

The Lady's Confession, p. 138

*Herein is our love made perfect, that we may
have boldness in the day of judgment: because
as he is, so are we in this world.*

1 John 4:17

Nothing is inexorable but love. Love is one, and love is changeless. For love loves into purity. Love has ever in view the absolute loveliness of that

24

which it beholds. Where loveliness is incomplete and love cannot love its fill of loving, it spends itself to make more lovely, that it may love more. It strives for perfection, even that itself may be perfected—not in itself, but in the object. There is nothing eternal but that which loves and can be loved, and love is ever climbing toward the consummation when such shall be the universe, imperishable, divine.

Discovering the Character of God, pp. 233–234;
Unspoken Sermons, First Series—"The Consuming Fire"

MAKE me a fellow worker with thee, Christ;
Nought else befits a God-born energy;
Of all that's lovely, only lives the highest,
Lifting the rest that it shall never die.
Up I would be to help thee—for thou liest
Not, linen-swathed in Joseph's garden-tomb,
But walkest crowned, Creation's heart and bloom.

Diary of an Old Soul, June 5

A LITTLE WONDER IS WORTH TONS OF KNOWLEDGE

AS WITH THE SKIRT OF HER MANTLE THE dark of the sunset wipes out the day, so with her sleep, the night makes a man fresh for the new day's journey. If it were not for sleep, the world could not go on. To feel the mystery of day and night, to gaze into the far receding spaces of their marvel, is more than to know all the facts of science and all the combinations of chemistry.

A little wonder is worth tons of knowledge in truly *knowing* what the universe means.

The Poet's Homecoming, p. 37

Therefore, behold, I will proceed to do a marvellous work among this people, even a marvellous work and a wonder: for the wisdom of their wise men shall perish, and the understanding of their prudent men shall be hid.
Isaiah 29:14

Behold ye among the heathen, and regard, and wonder marvellously: for I will work a work in your days, which ye will not believe, though it be told you.
Habakkuk 1:5

NAZARETH CARPENTER

THEN CAME A LITTLE STREAM AND THE horses splashed through it like children. Half a mile more and there was a sawmill with a mossy wheel, a pond behind dappled with sun and shade, a dark rush of water along a brown trough, and the air full of the sweet smell of sawn wood.

"Will you let me tell you, my lady, what this always makes me think of?" Malcolm said.

"What in particular do you mean?" returned Clementina coolly.

"This smell of new-sawn wood that fills the air."

She bowed her head in consent.

"It makes me think of Jesus in his father's workshop," said Malcolm, "how he must have smelled the same sweet scent of the trees of the world, broken for the uses of men; that is so sweet to me. Oh, my lady, it makes the earth very holy and very lovely to think that as we are in the world, so was he in the world. Oh, my lady, think! If God should be so nearly one with us that it was nothing strange to him thus to visit his people, then he is so entirely our Father that he cares even to death that we should understand and love him!"

The Marquis' Secret, p. 111

For we have not an high priest which cannot be touched with the feeling of our infirmities; but was in all points tempted like as we are, yet without sin.

Hebrews 4:15

THE GREATEST NEED OF THE HUMAN HEART

THE GRASSY BANK OF THE GENTLY FLOWING river was one of Robert's favorite haunts, and one Saturday afternoon in the end of July, when the westering sun was hotter than at midday, he went down to the lower end of a favorite field where the river was confined by a dam and plunged from the bank into the deep water. After a swim of half an hour, he ascended the higher part of the field and lay down to bask in the sun. In his ears was the hush rather than the rush of the water over the dam and the occasional murmur of a belt of trees that skirted the border of the field.

He lay gazing up into the depth of the sky, rendered deeper and bluer by the masses of white cloud that hung almost motionless below it. A gentle wind, laden with pine odors from the sun-heated trees behind him, flapped its light wing in his face. And all at once the humanity of the world smote his heart. The great sky towered up over him, and its divinity entered his soul; a strange longing after something "he knew not nor could name" awoke within him, followed by the pang of a sudden fear that there was no such thing as that which he sought.

Strange as it may sound to those who have never thought of such things except in connection with Sundays and Bibles and churches and sermons, that which was now working in Falconer's mind was the first dull and faint movement of the greatest need that the human heart possesses—the need of God. There must be truth in the scent of that pinewood; someone must mean it. There must be a glory in those heavens that depends not

upon our imagination; some power greater than they must dwell in them. Some spirit must move in that wind that haunts us with a kind of human sorrow; some soul must look up to us from the eye of that starry flower.

Little did Robert think that such was his need—that his soul was searching after One whose form was constantly presented to him, but as constantly obscured by the words without knowledge spoken in the religious assemblies of the land. Little did he realize that he was longing without knowing it on Saturday for that from which on the Sunday he would be repelled, again without knowing it. *The Musician's Quest, pp. 95–96*

This people draweth nigh unto me with their mouth, and honoureth me with their lips; but their heart is far from me. But in vain they do worship me, teaching for doctrines the commandments of men.
Matthew 15:8–9

The greatest obscuration of the words of the Lord comes from those who give themselves to interpret rather than do them. Theologians have done more to hide the Gospel of Christ than any of its adversaries. It was not for our understanding, but our will, that Christ came. He who does that which he sees, shall understand. He who is set upon understanding rather than doing, shall go on stumbling and mistaking and speaking foolishness.

Discovering the Character of God, pp. 199–200;
Unspoken Sermons, Second Series—"The Last Farthing"

REMEMBERING GOD

"DON'T YOU SOMETIMES FIND IT HARD TO remember God all through your work?" asked Clementina.

"I don't try to consciously remember him every moment. For he is in everything, whether I am thinking of it or not. When I go fishing, I go to catch God's fish. When I take Kelpie out for a ride, I am teaching one of God's wild creatures. When I read the Bible or Shakespeare, I am listening to the word of God, uttered in each after its own kind. When the wind blows on my face, it is God's wind." *The Marquis' Secret, p. 198*

In all things showing thyself a pattern of
good works: in doctrine showing
uncorruptness, gravity, sincerity, sound
speech, that cannot be condemned; that he
that is of the contrary part may be ashamed,
having no evil thing to say of you.
Titus 2:7–8

If we will but let our God and Father work his will with us, there can be no limit to his enlargement of our existence, to the flood of life with which he will overflow our consciousness. We have no conception of what life might be, of how vast the consciousness of which we could be made capable.

Discovering the Character of God, p. 22;
Unspoken Sermons, Second Series—"Life"

KINDNESS

KINDNESS WAS TO GIBBIE THE VERY MILK OF Mother Nature. Whose hand proffered it or what form it took, he cared no more than a stray kitten cares whether the milk set down to it be in a blue saucer or a white. But he always made the right return. The first thing a kindness deserves is acceptance, the next is transmission; Gibbie gave both without thinking much about either. For he never had taken a thought about what he should eat or what he should drink or wherewithal be clothed. *The Baronet's Song, p. 26*

*Therefore I say unto you, Take no thought
for your life, what ye shall eat, or what ye
shall drink; nor yet for your body, what ye
shall put on. Is not the life more than meat,
and the body than raiment?*
Matthew 6:25

The things of the world so crowd our hearts that there is no room in them for the things of God's heart, which would raise ours above all fear and make us merry children in our Father's house. How many whispers of the watching Spirit do we let slip by, while we brood over a need not yet come to us! Tomorrow makes today's whole head sick, its whole heart faint. When we should be still, sleeping or dreaming, we are fretting about an hour that lies half a sun's journey away!

Knowing the Heart of God, p. 80;
Unspoken Sermons, Second Series—"The Cause of Spiritual Stupidity"

YOU CANNOT BE CONVINCED THERE IS NO GOD

THERE ARE THOSE, LIKE GEORGE BASCOMBE, who believe men will be happy to learn there is no God. To them I would say, preach it then, and prosper in proportion to its truth. No; that from my pen would be a curse. Do not preach it until you have searched all the expanse of the universe, lest what you should consider a truth should turn out to be false and there should be after all somewhere, somehow, a living God, a Truth indeed who has created and governs the universe. You may be convinced there is no God such as this or that in whom men *imagine* they believe. But you cannot be convinced there is no God.   *The Curate's Awakening, p. 40*

And ye shall seek me, and find me, when ye
shall search for me with all your heart.
Jeremiah 29:13

Faith is not the fervent setting of the mind on "believing" for such-and-such an outcome—more often than not a desire generated by the man's own soul—as if *we*, and not God, were the originators and initiators of faith by the strength of our passions, the fervor of our prayers, and the forcefulness of our mental processes. True faith, rather, is that which, knowing the Lord's will, goes and does it, or, not knowing it, stands and waits, con-

tent in ignorance as in knowledge, because God wills. Faith neither presses into the hidden future, nor is careless of the knowledge that opens the path of action.

Man's first business is, "What does God want me to do?" not "What will God do if I do so and so?"   *Knowing the Heart of God, pp. 274–275;*

Unspoken Sermons, First Series—"The Temptation in the Wilderness"

FASTER no step moves God because the fool
Shouts to the universe God there is none;
The blindest man will not preach out the sun,
Though on his darkness he should found a school.
It may be, when he finds he is not dead,
Though world and body, sight and sound are fled,
Some eyes may open in his foolish head.

Diary of an Old Soul, June 13

A Man Is a Man No Matter How Far He Is from Manhood

VAVASOR REMAINED THE NEXT TWO WEEKS AT Yrndale. In those days Nature had the best chance with him she had ever had. For a man is a man however he may have been injured by society trying to substitute itself for both God and Nature. A man is potentially a man no matter how far he may be from actual manhood. Who knows what may not sometimes be awakened in a man when placed under the right influences.

During that fortnight, sensations came upon Vavasor of which he had never been aware. The most remarkable event of the time was that one morning he got up in time to see—and *for the purpose of seeing*—the sun rise. It was a great stride forward.

And that was not all: he really enjoyed it! He had poetry enough to feel something of the indwelling greatness that belonged to the vision itself. He felt a power of some kind present to his soul in the sight—though he counted it merely as a poetic feeling. It was, in fact, the drawing of the eternal nature in him toward God, of whom he knew so little.   *The Gentlewoman's Choice, pp. 88–89*

*For the invisible things of him from the
creation of the world are clearly seen, being
understood by the things that are made, even
his eternal power and Godhead; so that they
are without excuse.*
Romans 1:20

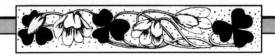

A GLORIOUS NEW DAY

WHAT A MORNING DAWNED AFTER THE storm! All night the lightning had been flashing itself into peace, and gliding farther and farther away. Bellowing and growling, the thunder had crept with it; but long after it could no more be heard, the lightning kept gleaming up, as if from a sea of flame behind the horizon.

The sun brought a glorious day, and seemed larger and mightier than before. To Helen, as she gazed eastward from her window, he seemed ascending his lofty pulpit to preach the story of the day named after him—the story of the Son-day. He testified to the rising again in splendor of the buried Son of the universe, with whom all the worlds and their hearts and suns arose. A light stream was floating up from the grass and the raindrops were sparkling everywhere. *The Lady's Confession, p. 138*

And very early in the morning the first day of the week, they came unto the sepulchre at the rising of the sun. And they said among themselves, Who shall roll us away the stone from the door of the sepulchre? And when they looked, they saw that the stone was rolled away: for it was very great. And entering into the sepulchre, they saw a young man sitting on the right side, clothed in a long white garment; and they were affrighted. And he saith unto them, Be not affrighted: Ye seek Jesus of Nazareth, which was crucified: he is risen; he is not here.

Mark 16:2–6

SOMEONE TO SAY MUST TO ME

"AH," SHE SAID, AND LOOKED UP INTO THE wide sky, "I should like to see the one who made all that. Think of knowing the very person who made that poor pigeon, and has got it now, and Miss Brown, and the wind. I must find him! He can't have made me and not care when I ask him to speak to me."

Richard said nothing in reply. They went walking toward the house and were silent. The moon went on with her silentness; she never stops being silent. When they came near the house, they fell to walking slower, but neither knew it. Barbara spoke again.

"Just imagine," she said, "if God were all the time at our backs, giving us one lovely thing after another, trying to make us look around and see who it was that was so good to us! Imagine him standing there wondering when his little one would look round and see him. If only I had him to love! Just think of all the shapes and lights and shadows and colors, and the moon and the wind and the water, all the creatures and the people."

There was another pause.

"I think I want someone to say *must* to me, someone to obey," she said at length. "I feel as if—"

There she stopped. Richard said nothing. They walked on a little farther before saying good night and parting.

As they went their separate ways, Richard was saying to himself that there could not be such a God as she spoke of.

But Barbara was saying to herself, "What if he *has* shown himself to me some time—one of those nights,

perhaps, when I was out till the sun rose—and I didn't know him! How frightful if there should be nobody up there at all—nobody anywhere!"

But in truth the God who knows *how not* to reveal himself must also know how *best* to reveal himself! If there be a calling child, there must be an answering father! Though her heart had, without knowing it, been calling toward him for years, now Barbara's mind began calling too; she knew she had to believe in God or die.

The Baron's Apprenticeship, pp. 79–80

Call unto me, and I will answer thee, and
shew thee great and mighty things, which
thou knowest not.
Jeremiah 33:3

God does not, by the instant gift of his Spirit, make us always feel right, desire good, love purity, aspire after him and his will. The reason he doesn't must be, therefore, either because he will not, or he cannot. If he will not, it must be because it would not be well to do so. If he cannot, then he would not if he could.

The truth is this: He wants to make us in his own image, *choosing* the good, *refusing* the evil. How could he effect this if he were *always* moving us from within? God gives us room *to be*. He does not oppress us with his will. He "stands away from us," that we may act from ourselves, that we may exercise the pure will for good.

Knowing the Heart of God, p. 301;
Unspoken Sermons, First Series—"The Eloi"

THE ETERNAL JOY OF THE UNIVERSE

IT WAS A LOVELY MORNING IN SUMMER. THE sun was but a little way above the horizon, and the dew-drops seemed to have come scattering from him as he shook his locks when he rose. The foolish larks were up, of course, for they fancied, come what might of winter and rough weather, the universe was founded in eternal joy, and themselves were endowed with the best of all rights to be glad, for there was the gladness inside, and struggling to get outside of them. And out it was coming in a divine profusion!

How many baskets would not have been needed to gather up the lordly waste of those scattered songs! In all the trees, in all the flowers, in every grassblade, and every weed, the sun was warming and coaxing and sooth-ing life into higher life.

And in those two on the path through the fields outside Testbridge, the same sun, light from the Father of lights, was nourishing highest life of all, that for the sake of which the Lord came, that he might set it growing in hearts of whose existence it was the very root.

A Daughter's Devotion, pp. 313–314

Every good gift and every perfect gift is from above, and cometh down from the Father of lights, with whom is no variableness, neither shadow of turning.
James 1:17

THE STORY OF GOD'S UNIVERSE

I WISH IT WERE POSSIBLE TO SEE THE MIND of a woman grow as she sits spinning or weaving: it would reveal the process next highest to creation. But the only hope of ever understanding such things lies in growing oneself.

There is the still growth of the moonlit night of reverie. Cloudy, with wind and a little rain, comes the morning of thought when the mind grows faster and the heart more slowly. Then wakes the storm in the forest of the human soul when it enlarges itself by great bursts of vision and leaps of understanding and resolve. Then floats up the mystic twilight eagerness, when the soul is driven toward that which is before, grasping at it with all the hunger of the new birth.

The story of God's universe lies in the growth of the individual soul. Kirsty's growth had been as yet quiet and steady. *The Peasant Girl's Dream, p. 26*

And he said, Whereunto shall we liken the kingdom of God? or with what comparison shall we compare it? It is like a grain of mustard seed, which, when it is sown in the earth, is less than all the seeds that be in the earth: But when it is sown, it groweth up, and becometh greater than all herbs, and shooteth out great branches; so that the fowls of the air may lodge under the shadow of it.
Mark 4:30–32

A SPIRIT OF PROPHECY

A SPIRIT OF PROPHECY, WHETHER FROM THE Lord or not, was abroad this summer in Glamerton. Those who read their Bibles took to reading the prophecies, all the prophecies, and scarcely anything but the prophecies. Either for himself or following in the track of his spiritual instructor, every man exercised his individual powers of interpretation upon these shadowy glimpses into the future. Whatever was known, whether about ancient Assyria or modern Tahiti, found its theoretical place.

Of course the Church of Rome received her due share of the curses from all parties. And neither the Church of England, the Church of Scotland, nor either of the dissenting sects went without its portion freely dealt, each of the last finding something that applied to all the rest. One might have thought they were reveling in the idea of vengeance, instead of striving for the rescue of their neighbors from the wrath to come.

The Maiden's Bequest, p. 175

*We have also a more sure word of prophecy;
whereunto ye do well that ye take heed, as
unto a light that shineth in a dark place, until
the day dawn, and the day star arise in your
hearts: Knowing this first, that no prophecy
of the scripture is of any private
interpretation. For the prophecy came not in
old time by the will of man: but holy men of
God spake as they were moved by the Holy
Ghost.*
2 Peter 1:19—21

THE DEEPEST TRUTH OF AN EVIL THEOLOGY

NOW AROSE WITHIN HIM THE EVIL IMAGES of a theology which explained all God's doings from a low rather than a lofty base. In such a system, hell is invariably the deepest truth, and the love of God is not so deep as hell. Hence, as often as a thought of religious duty arose in the mind of young Robert Falconer, it appeared in the form of escaping hell.

He was told that God was just, punishing those who did not go through a certain process of mind which it was impossible they should go through without help from him. This help he gave to some and withheld from others. And this God, they also added, was love.

It was logically absurd, of course, yet they continued to say God was love and many of them succeeded in believing it. Still, the article of God's harsh justice was the characteristic of his nature they taught chiefly to their children. No one dreamed of saying that nobody can do without the help of the Father any more than a newborn babe could of itself live and grow to be a man. No one said that out of the loving fatherhood of God the world was made and that God lives and loves infinitely more than the most loving man or woman on earth. *The Musician's Quest, pp. 60–61*

*The Lord is not slack concerning his
promise . . . but is longsuffering to us-ward,
not willing that any should perish, but that
all should come to repentance.*

2 Peter 3:9

THE IDEA OF GOD
GROWS SLOWLY

MANY AND LONG WERE THE CONVERSA-
tions between the two girls when everyone else was
asleep. And now the teaching for which Euphra had
longed sprang in a fountain at her own door. It had been
near her all along, but she had not known it, for its hour
had not come. Now she drank as only the thirsty drink.

The second night Margaret came to Euphra's room,
she said, "Shall I tell you about my father tonight?"

Euphra was delighted.

So they sat down and Margaret began to talk about
her childhood, the cottage she lived in, the fir wood and
all around it, the work she used to do. Summer and
winter, springtime and harvest, storm and sunshine all
came into the tale. Her mother came into it and the
grand form of her father. Every time Euphra saw him
thus in the mirror of Margaret's memory, she saw him
more clearly than before. Sometimes she asked a question or two, but generally she allowed Margaret's words
to flow unchecked, for she painted her pictures better
when the colors did not dry between. They talked on
far into the night. At length Margaret stopped suddenly
and looked at the clock on the chimney-piece.

"I have kept you up too late! I must get you to bed."

"You will come tomorrow night again?"

"Yes, I will."

"Then I will go to bed like a good child," said Euphra,
smiling.

The next night, Margaret spoke again of her father
and what he taught her. Euphra had thought much about
him, and every fresh touch which the story gave to the

portrait allowed her to know him better. But what is most worthy of record is that ever as the picture of David grew on the vision of Euphra, the idea of God was growing unawares upon her inward sight. She was learning more and more about his character from the character of his servant. Faith came of itself, and slowly grew.

The Tutor's First Love, p. 202

So then faith cometh by hearing, and hearing
by the word of God.
Romans 10:17

But without faith it is impossible to please
him: for he that cometh to God must believe
that he is, and that he is a rewarder of them
that diligently seek him.
Hebrews 11:6

Not the lovingest heart that ever beat can even reflect the length and breadth and depth and height of that love of God, which shows itself in his Son—one, and of one mind, with himself. The whole history is a divine agony to give divine life to creatures. The outcome of that agony, the victory of that creative and again creative energy, will be radiant life, the flower of which is joy unspeakable. Every child will look into the eyes of the Father, and the eyes of the Father will receive the child with an infinite embrace.

Discovering the Character of God, p. 89;
Unspoken Sermons, Second Series—"Life"

THOROUGH AND IDEAL LOVE

GIBBIE'S LOVE WAS SIMPLE, UNSELFISH, undemanding—not merely asking for no return but asking for no recognition, requiring not even that its existence should be known. He was a rare one, who did not make the common mistake of confusing the desire to be loved, with love itself.

Some would count worthless the love of a man who loved everybody. There would be no distinction in being loved by such a man!—and distinction, as a guarantee of their own great worth is what such seek. There are women who desire to be the sole object of a man's affection, and are all their lives devoured by unlawful jealousies. A love that had never gone forth upon human being but themselves would be to them the treasure to sell all that they might buy. And the man who brought such a love might in truth be all-absorbed therein himself.

The poorest of creatures may well be absorbed in the poorest of loves. The man who loves most will love best. The man who thoroughly loves God and his neighbor is the only man who will love a woman ideally—who can love her with the love God thought of between them when he made man male and female.

The Baronet's Song, p. 199

Husbands, love your wives, even as Christ
also loved the church, and gave himself for it.
Ephesians 5:25

TRUST WORK, NOT MONEY

AT EVERY STREAM HE CAME TO HE BATHED his feet. He had no certain goal, though he knew his direction and was in no haste. He had confidence in God and in his own powers as the gift of God, and knew that wherever he went he need not be hungry long, even should the little money in his pocket be spent.

It is better to trust in work than in money. God never buys anything, and is forever at work. Donal was now descending the heights of youth to walk along the king's highroad of manhood. He had lost his past—that of a shepherd and a student—but so as not to be ashamed. His future was now before him. *The Shepherd's Castle, p. 11*

If riches increase,
set not your heart upon them.
Psalms 62:10

The soul in harmony with his Maker has more life, a larger being, than the soul consumed with cares. The sage has a larger life than the clown. The poet is more alive than the man whose life flows out that money may come in. The man who loves his fellow is infinitely more alive than he whose endeavor is to exalt himself above his neighbor. The man who strives to be better in his being is more alive than he who longs for praise.

Discovering the Character of God, p. 21,
Unspoken Sermons, Second Series—"Life"

45

HE IS YOUR FATHER, WHETHER YOU WISH IT OR NOT

"NO, I COULD NOT TELL MY FATHER OF IT. But I could leave it to God. I could trust God with what I could not speak to my father about. He is my father's Father, and so more to him and me than we could be to each other. I loved my father ten times more because he loved God, and because God had secrets with him."

"I wish God were a Father to me as he is to you, Margaret."

"But he is your Father, whether you wish it or not. He cannot be more your Father than he is. You may be more his child than you are, but not more than he meant you to be nor more than he made you for. You are infinitely more his child than you have grown to yet. He made you altogether his child, but you have not given in to it yet."

Euphra made no answer, but wept. Margaret said no more. *The Tutor's First Love, p. 206*

*And because ye are sons, God hath sent forth
the Spirit of his Son into your hearts, crying,
Abba, Father.*
Galatians 4:6

*There is one body, and one Spirit, even as ye
are called in one hope of your calling; One
Lord, one faith, one baptism, One God and*

Father of all, who is above all, and through
all, and in you all.
Ephesians 4:4–6

God is our Father all the time, for he is true. But until we respond with the truth of children, he cannot fully reveal the Father to us; there is no place for the dove of tenderness to alight. He is our Father, but we are not yet his children. Because we are not his children, we must become his sons and daughters. Nothing else will satisfy him, or us, until we be one with our Father!

Discovering the Character of God, p. 226;
Unspoken Sermons, Second Series—"Abba, Father!"

I AM lost before thee, Father! Yet I will
Claim of thee my birthright ineffable.
Thou lay'st it on me, son, to claim thee, sire;
To that which thou hast made me, I aspire;
To thee, the sun, upflames thy kindled fire.
No man presumes in that to which he was born;
Less than the gift to claim, would be the giver to scorn.

Diary of an Old Soul, June 10

THOUGHT AND FEELING

SUCH WAS THE AVIDITY AND GROWING intelligence with which the little, naked town savage listened to what Donal read to him that his presence added to Donal's own live soul of thought and feeling. From listening to his own lips through Gibbie's ears, he not only understood many things better but, perceiving what things must puzzle Gibbie, came sometimes to his astonishment to see that, in fact, he did not understand them himself.

Thus the bond between the boy and the child grew closer—even though Donal imagined now and then that Gibbie might be a creature of some speechless race other than human. *The Baronet's Song, p. 59*

*And we know that the Son of God is come,
and hath given us an understanding, that we
may know him that is true, and we are in him
that is true, even in his Son Jesus Christ.*
1 John 5:20

The obedient Jesus is Jesus, the Truth.

He is true and the root of all truth and development of truth in men. Their very being, however far from the true human, is the undeveloped Christ in them, and his likeness to Christ is the truth of a man, even as the perfect meaning of a flower is the truth of a flower. *Discovering the Character of God, p. 68, Unspoken Sermons, Third Series—"The Truth"*

Shame in Making Apology or Shame in Doing Wrong

Forgue's anger began to rise once more, but he controlled himself. He was evidently at strife with himself: he knew he was wrong but could not bring himself to say so. It is one of the poorest of human weaknesses that a man would be ashamed of saying he has done wrong instead of so ashamed of having done wrong that he cannot rest till he has said so. For the shame cleaves fast until the confession removes it.

He walked away a step or two and stood with his back to Donal, poking the point of his stick into the grass. All at once he turned and said, "I will apologize if you will tell me one thing. Why did you not return either of my blows yesterday?"

"Because to do so would have been to disobey the instructions I am under."

"I only wanted to know it was not cowardice; I could not make an apology to a coward."

"If I were a coward, you would owe me an apology all the same, and he is a poor creature who will not pay his debts. But I hope it will not be necessary I should ever have to convince you I have no fear of you."

The Shepherd's Castle, pp. 48–49

See that none render evil for evil unto any man; but ever follow that which is good, both among yourselves, and to all men.
1 Thessalonians 5:15

NOTHING PLEASES GOD LIKE THE TRUTH

"IT'S MORE FOR OUR SAKES THAN HIS OWN that God cares about his glory. I don't believe that he thinks about his glory except for the sake of truth and men's hearts dying for the lack of it."

Mrs. Falconer thought for a moment. "It may be that you're right, laddie, but you have a way of saying things that is some fearsome."

"God's not like a proud man to take offense, Grannie. There's nothing that pleases him like the truth, and there's nothing that displeases him like lying, particularly when it's pretended praise. He wants no false praising. Now, *you* say things about him sometimes that sound fearsome to me."

"What kind of things, laddie?" asked the old lady, with offense glooming in the background.

"Like when you speak of him as if he was a poor, proud man, full of his own importance and ready to be down on anybody that didn't call him by the name of his office—always thinking about his own glory, instead of the quiet, mighty, grand, self-forgetting, all-creating, loving being that he is. Eh, Grannie! Think of the face of that man of sorrows, that never said a hard word to a sinful woman or a despised publican. Was he thinking about his own glory, do you think? And whatever isn't like Christ isn't like God."

"But laddie, Christ came to satisfy God's justice by suffering the punishment due to our sins, to turn aside his wrath and curse. So Jesus couldn't be *altogether* God."

"Oh, but he is, Grannie. He came to satisfy God's justice by giving him back his children, by making them

see that God was just, by sending them back home to fall at his feet. He came to lift the weight of the sins off the shoulders of them that did them by making them turn against the sin and toward God. And there isn't a word of reconciling God to us in the New Testament, for there was no need of that; it was *us* that needed to be reconciled to him. And so he bore our sins and carried our sorrows, for those sins caused him no end of grief of mind and pain in his body. It wasn't his own sins or God's wrath that caused him suffering, but our own sins. And he took them away. He took our sins upon him, for he came into the middle of them and took them up—by no sleight of hand, by no quibbling of the preachers about imputing his righteousness to us and such like. But he took them and took them away, and here am I, Grannie, growing out of my sins in consequence, and there are you, growing out of yours in consequence, too."

"I wish that may be true, laddie. But I don't care how you put it," returned his grandmother, bewildered no doubt, "just so long as you put him first and say with all your heart, 'His will be done!'"

"His will be done, Grannie," responded Robert readily.   *The Musician's Quest, pp. 199–200*

*For though I would desire to glory, I shall
not be a fool; for I will say the truth: but now
I forbear, lest any man should think of me
above that which he seeth me to be, or that he
heareth of me.*
2 Corinthians 12:6

Smoked Glass Held Up in Front of God

THE KEEN CONSCIENCE OF THE GIRL HAD made her very early turn herself towards the quarter where the sun ought to rise. Unhappily, she had not gone direct to the very word of the Master himself.

How could she? From very childhood her mind had been filled with traditional utterances concerning the divine character and the divine plans—the merest inventions of men far more desirous of understanding what they were required to understand than of doing what they were required to do.

She had had a governess of the so-called orthodox type, a large proportion of whose teaching was of the worst kind of heresy, for it was lies against him who is light. Her doctrines were so many smoked glasses held up between the mind of her pupil and the glory of the living God—such as she would have seen for herself in time had she gone to the only knowable truth concerning God, the face of Jesus Christ. Had she set herself to understand him, she would have neither believed these things nor taught them to her little pupil.

The Shepherd's Castle, p. 53

Whosoever therefore shall break one of these least commandments, and shall teach men so, he shall be called the least in the kingdom of heaven: but whosoever shall do and teach them, the same shall be called great in the kingdom of heaven.
Matthew 5:19

THE COMPULSION TO SEEK HELP

FOR EUPHRA'S MISERY THERE WERE VERY sufficient reasons. Her continued lameness gave her great cause for anxiety. But worse still, her mind had been thrown back upon itself as often happens in loneliness and suffering.

Simple natures will often look up at once, lifting their eyes to the heavens whence comes their aid. Yet Euphra was of a nature that will endure an immense amount of misery before it feels compelled to look for help whence all help and healing comes. But even Euphra was cast down so low in her despair that she had begun to look upward, for the waters were about to close over her head. She had therefore taken herself to the one man of whom she heard knew God. She wrote, but no answer came. Days and days passed, but there was no reply.

In bitterness she said to herself, "If I cried to God forever I should hear no word of reply. What does he care for me?"

Yet even as she spoke, she rose and by a sudden impulse threw herself on the floor and cried out, for the first time, "O God, help me."   *The Tutor's First Love, p. 179*

*Behold, for peace I had great bitterness: but
thou hast in love to my soul delivered it from
the pit of corruption: for thou hast cast all
my sins behind thy back.*
Isaiah 38:17

WHAT DOTH EVERY SIN DESERVE?

EVERY SATURDAY MURDOCH MALISON'S pupils had to learn a certain number of questions from the Shorter Catechism, with their corresponding proofs from Scripture. Whoever failed in the task was condemned to imprisonment for the remainder of the day or until the task was accomplished. On one Saturday each month, moreover, the students were tested on all the questions and proofs that had been covered during the previous month.

The day in question was one of those of accumulated labor, and the only proof Alec Forbes had succeeded in displaying was proof of his inability for the task. In consequence he was condemned to be kept in—a trial hard indeed for one whose chief delights were the open air and the active exertion of his growing body.

Seeing his downcast expression filled Annie with such concern that she lost track of the class and did not know when her turn came until suddenly the master was standing before her in silent expectation. He had approached soundlessly and then stood till the universal silence had at length aroused Annie's consciousness. Then with a smile on his thin lips, but a lowering thundercloud on his brow, he repeated the question: "What doth every sin deserve?"

Annie, bewildered and burning with shame at finding herself the core of the silence, could not recall a word of the answer given in the Catechism. So in her confusion she fell back on her common sense and experience.

"What doth every sin deserve?" repeated the tyrant.

"A lickin'," whimpered Annie, her eyes filling with tears.

The Maiden's Bequest, p. 47

*That as sin hath reigned unto death, even so
might grace reign through righteousness unto
eternal life by Jesus Christ our Lord.*
Romans 5:21

How terribly have the theologians misrepresented God's character. They represent him as a great king on a huge throne, thinking how grand he is, and making it the business of his being and the end of his universe to keep up his glory, wielding the bolts of a Jupiter against them that take his name in vain.

But how contrary this is to what the Gospel accounts plainly tell us. Brothers, sisters, have you found our King? There he is, kissing little children and saying they are like God. There he is at the table with the head of a fisherman lying on his chest, and somewhat heavy at heart that even he, the beloved disciple, cannot yet understand him well. The simplest peasant who loves his children and his sheep would be the true type of our God beside that monstrosity of a monarch.

Discovering the Character of God, pp. 31–32;
Unspoken Sermons, First Series—"The Child in the Midst"

GREAT AND SMALL IN EVERY CLASS

As HE STOOD UP HE DISPLAYED A FINE, powerful frame, over six feet in height, and perfectly poised. With a great easy stride he swept silently out of the shop. Neither from his gait nor his look would one have guessed that he had been all day at work on the remnant of property he could still call his own.

To an English gentleman it would have seemed strange that one who had come from such a line of patriarchal ancestors, and who held the land of the country, should talk with such familiarity with a girl in a humble little shop in a most miserable hamlet. It would have seemed stranger yet that such a man should toil at the labor the soul of a gentleman despises.

But there are great and small in every class—here and there a ploughman who understands the poets, here and there a large-minded shopkeeper, and here and there an unselfish duke. Less worldly *cleverness* is required for country affairs, and so they leave more room for thinking. Doubtless many of the youth's ancestors would likewise have held such labor unworthy of a gentleman. But this, the last Macruadh, was not like most of his pedigree, and had now and then a peep into the kingdom of heaven. *The Highlander's Last Song, p. 28*

*Humble yourselves in the sight of the Lord,
and he shall lift you up.*
James 4:10

I Cannot Say What You Should Do

"BUT, MR. FALCONER," THE LADY ASKED, "YOU still have not given an answer to the question I posed. What exactly *is* one's duty?"

"The thing that lies next to you, of course. You can be the sole judge of that."

"Should I go out into the city, as you do?"

"I simply cannot say what *you* should do. But sit down and count the cost before you do any mischief by beginning what you are unfit for. Last week I was compelled more than once to leave the house where my duty led me, so sick I could not function. The room I was in was crowded with human animals, and at least one dying."

A mist was gathering over the lady's eyes.

"And you must spend time preparing yourself. Our Savior himself had to be thirty years in the world before he had footing enough in it to begin to teach publicly. He had been laying the necessary foundations all the time. So few that are involved with churches or societies have the knowledge of the poor that I have. Many of them could do something if they would only set about it simply, and not be so anxious to convert them, if they would allow themselves to be their friends."

The Musician's Quest, p. 227

The Son of man came eating and drinking, and they say, Behold a man gluttonous, and a winebibber, a friend of publicans and sinners. But wisdom is justified of her children.
Matthew 11:19

WE MUST BE BEFORE WE CAN DO

HESTER WENT TO HER ROOM AND BEGAN thinking again.

She was one of those women who, from the very first dawn of consciousness, have all their lives tried, with varying degrees of success, to do the right thing. But she was young and did not consider herself as caring as she wanted to be, and was frequently irritated by her failure; for it is impossible to satisfy the hard master *self*. While he flatters some, he requires of others more than they can give.

God seems to take pleasure in working by degrees. The progress of the truth is as the permeation of leaven, or the growth of a seed: a multitude of successive small sacrifices may work more good in the world than many a large one. What would even our Lord's death on the cross have been except as the crown of a life in which he died daily, giving himself, soul, body, and spirit, to his men and women? It is the *being* that is precious. Being is the mother to all little *doings* as well as the grown-up *deeds* and the mighty heroic *sacrifice*.

Hester had not had time, neither had she prayed enough to be yet, though she was growing well toward it. She was a good way up the hill, and the Lord was coming down to meet her, but they had not quite met yet so as to go up the rest of the way together.

What had gradually been rising in Hester was the feeling that she must not waste her life! She must *do* something! Her deep awareness of the misery around her told her she should do something to help those in need. But what? *The Gentlewoman's Choice, p. 26*

Being confident of this very thing, that he
which hath begun a good work in you will
perform it until the day of Jesus Christ.
Philippians 1:6

No man or woman can yet do what Christ tells him aright. But are you trying? Obedience is not perfection, but making an effort. He never gave a commandment knowing it was of no use for it could not be done. He tells us to do only things that *can* be done. He tells us a thing knowing that we must do it, or be lost. Not even his Father himself could save us but by getting us at length to do everything he commands, for there is no other way to know life, to know the holy secret of divine being.

He knows that you can try, and that in your trying and failing he will be able to help you, until at length you will do the will of God even as he does it himself. He takes the will in the imperfect deed, and makes the deed at last perfect.

The most correct notions without obedience are worthless. The doing of the will of God is the way to oneness with God.

Knowing the Heart of God, p. 33;
Unspoken Sermons, Second Series—"The Truth in Jesus"

A PLACE TO THINK

AT FIVE THE SCHOOL WAS DISMISSED FOR the day, but not without another prayer. A succession of jubilant shouts arose as the boys rushed out into the street. Every day to them was a cycle of strife, suffering, and deliverance. Birth and death, with the life struggle between, were shadowed out in it. The difference was this: the stone-hearted God of popular theology in the person of Murdoch Malison ruled the world, and not the God revealed in the man Christ Jesus. Most of them, having felt the day more or less a burden, were now going home to heaven for the night.

Annie, having no home, was among the few exceptions. Dispirited and hopeless—a terrible condition for a child—she wondered how Alec Forbes could be so merry.

She had but one comfort left: hopefully, no one would prevent her from creeping up to her own desolate garret, which was now the dreary substitute for Brownie's stall. There the persecuting boys were not likely to follow her. And if the rats were in the garret, so was the cat—or at least the cat knew the way to it. There she might think in peace about some things she never had to think about before. *The Maiden's Bequest, p. 38*

Let the proud be ashamed; for they dealt perversely with me without a cause: but I will meditate in thy precepts.
Psalms 119:78

DENYING IT OR DENYING HIM?

"IS DUTY TOWARD GOD SUCH A PRACTICAL matter with you, Florimel, that you cannot listen to anything he has got to say about it?" asked Clementina.

Florimel shrugged her shoulders.

"For my part, I would give all I have to know there was a God worth believing in."

"Clementina!"

"What?"

"Of course there's a God. It is very horrible to deny it."

"Which is worse—to deny *it* or to deny *him*? Now, I confess to doubting *it*—that is, the very fact of a God. But you seem to me to deny God himself, for you admit there is a God—think it very wicked to deny that—and yet you don't take interest enough in him to wish to learn anything about him. You won't *think*, Florimel. I don't fancy you ever really *think*."

The Marquis' Secret, pp. 138–139

For men shall be lovers of their own
selves, . . . heady, highminded, lovers of
pleasures more than lovers of God; having a
form of godliness, but denying the power
thereof: from such turn away.
2 Timothy 3:2–5

THE INFLUENCE
OF ANCESTORS

LADY ARCTURA LED THE WAY, AND DONAL followed up the main staircase to the second floor and into the small, curious room, evidently one of the oldest in the castle. Inside, it was very charming with the oddest nooks and corners, recesses and projections.

Donal cast round his eyes. Turning to Lady Arctura he said, "I feel as if I were here searching into a human nature. A house looks always to me so like a mind—full of strange, inexplicable shapes at first sight, which gradually arrange, disentangle, and explain themselves as you go on to know them. In all houses there are places we know nothing about yet, just as in our own selves."

"It is a very old house," said Arctura; "so many hands have been employed in the building through so many generations."

"That is true, but where the house continues in the same family, the builders have transmitted their nature as well as their house to those who come after them."

"Then you think," said Arctura, almost with a shudder, "that I cannot but inherit from my ancestors a nature like the house they have left me? That the house is a fit outside to my inner nature—as the shell fits the snail?"

"Yes, probably so, but with an infinite power to modify the relation. Everyone is born nearer to God than to any ancestor, and so it rests with everyone to cultivate either the godlikeness in him, or his ancestral nature—to choose whether he will be of God, or those that have gone before him in the way of the world."

"That seems to me very strange doctrine," murmured Arctura in some uncertainty.

"It is, however, unavoidably true that we inherit from our ancestors tendencies to both vices and virtues. That which was a vice indulged in by my great-great-grandfather possibly may be in me a tendency to the same or a similar vice."

"Oh, how horrible!" cried Arctura.

"We need God not the more, but we know the better how much we need him," said Donal. "In you they are not vices—only possibilities which cannot become vices until they are obeyed. It rests with the man to destroy in himself even the possibility of them by opening the door to him who knocks. Then, again, there are all kinds of counteracting and redeeming influences in opposite directions. Perhaps, wherein the said ancestor was most wicked, his wife, from whom is the descent as much as from him, was especially lovely. The ancestor may, for instance, have been cruel, and the ancestress as tender as the hen that gathers her chickens under her wing. The danger, in an otherwise even nature, is of being caught in some sudden gust of unsuspected passionate impulse and carried away of the one tendency before the other has time to assert and the will to rouse itself."

"You comfort me a little."

"And then you must remember," continued Donal, "that nothing in its immediate root is evil; that sometimes it is from the best human roots that the worst things spring, just because the conscience and the will have not been brought to bear upon them."

The Shepherd's Castle, pp. 179–180

Choose you this day whom ye will serve, . . .
but as for me and my house, we will serve the
Lord.
Joshua 24:15

THE STIRRING
OF HEARTS

"IT'S A SHILLING, SIR," SHE SAID, LOOKING UP at him with the coin lying on her open palm.

"Well, Annie," said the old man, suddenly elevated into prophecy for the child's need, "when God offers us a sixpence, it may turn out to be two. Good night, my bairn."

But Mr. Cowie was sorely dissatisfied with himself. For not only did he perceive that the heart of the child could not thus be satisfied, but he began to feel something new stirring in his own heart. The fact was that in her own way Annie was further along than Mr. Cowie. She was a child searching hard to find the face of her Father in heaven: he was but one of God's babies, who had been receiving contently and happily the good things God gave him but never looking up to find the eyes of him from whom the good gifts came.

And now the heart of the man, touched by the motion of the child's heart—yearning after the truth about her Father in heaven, and yet scarcely believing that he could be so good as her father on earth—began to stir uneasily within him. He went down on his knees and hid his face in his hands.   *The Maiden's Bequest, pp. 106–107*

But the hour cometh, and now is, when the
true worshippers shall worship the Father in
spirit and in truth: for the Father seeketh such
to worship him.
John 4:23

IGNORANCE—BOTH PUNISHMENT AND KINDNESS

THE TEACHINGS OF THE LORD ARE FOR THE understanding of the man only who is practical—who does the things he knows, who seeks to understand it practically. They reveal to the live conscience, otherwise not to the keenest intellect—though at the same time they may help to rouse the conscience with glimpses of the truth, where the man is on the borders of waking.

Ignorance may be at once a punishment and a kindness. "Because you will not *do*, you shall not *see*; but it would be worse for you if you did see, not being of the disposition to do."

God is visible all around us, but only to the man or woman who *would* see him.   *The Curate's Awakening, p.* 107

Blessed are the pure in heart:
for they shall see God.
Matthew 5:8

Man is man only in the doing of truth. In the fulfilling of his relations to his origin, he himself becomes a truth, a living truth. The man is true who chooses duty. Relations, truths, duties are shown to the man away beyond him, that he may choose them, and be a child of God, choosing righteousness like him.   *Discovering the Character of God, p.* 67;
Unspoken Sermons, Third Series—"The Truth"

THE PLACE OF MISERY

"FOR THE GLORY OF GOD, MR. SUTHERLAND, I would die the death. For the will of God I'm ready for anything he likes."

The almost passionate earnestness with which David spoke made it impossible for Hugh to reply at once. After a few moments he ventured to ask: "Would you do nothing that other people should know God, David?"

"Anything that he likes. But I wouldn't take to interfering with *his* design with *my* words. He's revealing himself from morning till night, from year's end to year's end."

"But you seem to make out that God is nothing but love."

"Ay, nothing but love. And why not?"

"Because we are told that he is just."

"Would he be just for long if he did not love us?" asked David.

"But doesn't he punish sin?"

"It would hardly be kindness if he didn't punish sin, not to use every means to put the evil thing far from us. Whatever may be meant by the place of misery, depend upon it, Mr. Sutherland, it's only another form of his love. Love shining through the fogs of evil, and thus made to look very different. Man, rather than see my Maggie—and you'll have no doubt that I love her— rather than see my Maggie do some wicked thing, I'd see her lying dead at my feet. But suppose once the wickedness is past, it's not at my feet I would lay her, but upon my heart with my old arms around her, to hold further wickedness away from her all the better. And

shall mortal man be more just than God? Shall a man be more pure than his Maker?" *The Tutor's First Love, pp. 37–38*

*To whom God would make known what is
the riches of the glory of this mystery among
the Gentiles; which is Christ in you, the hope
of glory.*
Colossians 1:27

The one supreme action of life possible to us is to give up our life.

Christ did it of himself, that we might be able to do it in ourselves, after him, through his originating act. But we must do it ourselves. The help that he has given and gives us every moment, is all there that we may, as we must, do it ourselves. Until then we are not alive.

When a man or woman truly and perfectly says with Jesus, and as Jesus said it, "Thy will be done," he closes the everlasting life-circle. The life of the Father and the Son flows through him; he is a part of the divine organism. Then is the prayer of the Lord in him fulfilled: "I in them and thou in me, that they may be made perfect in one."

Thy will, O God, be done!

*Discovering the Character of God, p. 187;
Unspoken Sermons, Third Series—"The Creation in Christ"*

THE MORE MANLY OCCUPATION

MARY DID NOT LEAVE HER SHOP, NOR DID Joseph leave his forge. Mary was proud of her husband, not merely because he was a musician, but because he was a blacksmith. She honored the manhood that could do hard work. The day will come when the youth of our country will recognize that it is a more manly thing to follow a good craft, if it makes the hands black as coal, than to spend the day in keeping books, and making accounts, and investing money, and making fortunes at the expense of other people. Of course from a higher point of view still, all work set by God and divinely done is of equal honor. But where there is a choice, I would gladly see a son of mine choose rather to be a blacksmith, a watchmaker, a bookbinder, a cobbler, a woodworker, than a banker or broker. *A Daughter's Devotion, p. 313*

Whether therefore ye eat, or drink, or
whatsoever ye do, do all to the glory of God.
1 Corinthians 10:31

The man who recognizes the truth of any human relation and neglects the duty involved is not a true man. . . . A man may be aware of the highest truths of many things, and yet not be a true man, inasmuch as the essentials of manhood are not his aim: he has not come into the flower of his own being.

Discovering the Character of God, p. 67;
Unspoken Sermons, Third Series—"The Truth"

THE TRUE MEASURING ROD

MR. WINGFOLD, MR. DREW, AND SOME others of the best men in the place did think Mr. Polwarth the greatest in the kingdom of heaven of those they knew. But Glaston was altogether of a different opinion. Which was the right opinion must be left to the measuring rod that shall be applied to the statures of men on the last day.

The history of the kingdom of heaven—need I say how very different a thing that is from what is called *church history?*—is the only history which will ever be able to be thoroughly written. It will not only explain itself, while doing so it will explain all other attempted histories as well. Many of those who will then be found first in this eternal record may have been insignificant in the eyes of their contemporaries—even their religious contemporaries. They may have been absolutely unknown to the generations that came after them, and yet were the real men and women of potency, who worked as light and as salt in the world.

When the real worth of things is the measuring rod of their esteem, then will the kingdom of our God and his Christ be at hand. *The Lady's Confession, p. 195*

Whosoever therefore shall humble himself as this little child, the same is greatest in the kingdom of heaven.
Matthew 18:4

HE WILL BE
WITH GOD

"IS IT A GOOD THING TO THINK SO MUCH about religion at your age?" asked Lady Joan. "There is a time for everything. You talk like one of those good little children in books that always die—at least I have heard of such books; I never read any of them."

Cosmo laughed again.

"Which of us is happier—you or me? The moment I saw you, I thought you looked like one that hadn't enough of something; but if you knew that the great beautiful person we call God was always near you, it would be impossible for you to go on being sad."

"But you can't mean that the people of this world should live apart from him who put them in it. He is all the same, in this world, and in every other. The thought of God fills me so full of life that I want to go and do something for everybody. I don't think I shall be miserable when my father dies."

"Oh, Cosmo! And with such a good father as yours! I am shocked!"

Cosmo turned and looked at her.

"Lady Joan," he said slowly, "if my father were taken from me, I should be so proud of him, I should have no room to be miserable. I cannot see him now, and yet I am glad because my father is—way down there in the old castle. And when he is gone from me, I shall be glad still, for he will be somewhere all the same—with God as he is now. We shall meet again one day, after all."

The Laird's Inheritance, pp. 136–137

*And ye now therefore have sorrow: but I will
see you again, and your heart shall rejoice,
and your joy no man taketh from you.*
John 16:22

The fire of God, which is his essential being, his love, his creative power, is a fire unlike its earthly symbol in this, that it is only at a distance it burns— that the farther from him, the worse it burns, and that when we turn and begin to approach him, the burning begins to change to comfort.

The glory of being, the essence of life and its joy, must, like the sun, consume the dead and send corruption down to the dust. That which it burns in the soul is not of the soul. Yet so close to the soul is the foul fungus growth sprung from and subsisting upon it, that the burning of it is felt through every spiritual nerve. When the evil parasites are consumed away, that is when the man yields his self and all that self's low world and returns to his Lord and God, then that which before he was aware of only as burning, he will feel as love, comfort, strength—an eternal, ever-growing life in him.   *Discovering the Character of God, p. 172;*

Unspoken Sermons, Second Series—"The Fear of God"

THE SECRET OF UNCERTAINTY

TO KNOW GOD IS TO BE IN THE SECRET place of all knowledge, and to trust him changes the whole outlook surrounding mystery and seeming contradictions and unanswered questions, from one of doubt or fear or bewilderment, to one of hope. The unknown may be some lovely truth in store for us, which we are not yet ready to apprehend. Not to be intellectually certain of a truth does not prevent the heart that loves and obeys that truth from getting the goodness out of it, from drawing life from it because it is loved, not because it is understood. *The Lady's Confession, pp. 229–230*

I have not spoken in secret, in a dark place of
the earth: I said not unto the seed of Jacob,
Seek ye me in vain: I the Lord speak
righteousness, I declare things that are right.
Isaiah 45:19

Doubts are the messengers of the Living One to rouse the honest heart. They are the first knock at our door of things that are not yet, but have to be, understood. Theirs in general is the inhospitable reception of angels who do not come in their own likeness.

Doubt must precede every deeper assurance. For uncertainties are what we first see when we look into a region hitherto unknown, unexplored, unannexed. *Discovering the Character of God, pp. 218–219;*
Unspoken Sermons, Second Series—"The Voice of Job"

THE WILL OF GOD IS ALL

THE WILL OF GOD WAS ALL WINGFOLD cared about, and if the church was not content with that, the church was nothing to him, and might do with him as it would. He gave himself altogether to the Lord, and therefore to his people. He believed in Jesus Christ as the everyday life of the world, whose presence is just as needed in bank or shop or House of Lords, as at what so many of the clergy call the altar.

When the Lord is known as the heart of every joy, as well as the refuge from every sorrow, then the altar will be known for what it is—an ecclesiastical antique. The Father permitted but never ordained sacrifice; in tenderness to his children he ordered the ways of their unbelieving belief.

So thought and said Wingfold, and if he did not say so in the pulpit, it was not for fear of his fellows regarding him as a heretic but because so few of his people would understand. He would spend no strength in trying to shore up the church; he sent his lifeblood through its veins, and his appeal to the Living One, for whose judgment he waited.   *The Baron's Apprenticeship, p. 117*

*Beloved, follow not that which is evil, but
that which is good. He that doeth good is of
God: but he that doeth evil hath not seen God.*
3 John 1:11

CASTLES THAT GOD BUILDS

"THE WORLD IS FULL OF LITTLE DEATHS— deaths of all sorts and sizes, rather let me say. For this one I was prepared. The good summer land calls you to its bosom, and you must go."

"Come with me!" cried Clementina.

"A man must not leave his work—however irksome—for the more peaceful pleasure," answered the schoolmaster.

"But I cannot do without you—not for long. Can't you come? I shall be traveling alone."

A shadow came over the schoolmaster's face. "I never do anything of myself. I go not where I wish, but where I seem to be called or sent. I used to build many castles, not without a certain beauty of their own—that is, when I was less understanding. Now I leave them to God to build for me: He does it better and they last longer. But I do not think he will keep me here for long, for I find I cannot do much for these children. This ministration I take to be more for my good than theirs—a little trial of faith and patience for me. True, I *might* be happier where I could hear the larks, but I do not know anywhere that I have been more peaceful than in this little room."

"It is not at all a fit place for *you*," said Clementina.

"Gently, my lady. It is a greater than thou that sets the bounds of my habitation. Perhaps he may give me a palace one day. But the Father has decreed for his children that they shall know the thing that is neither their ideal nor his. All in his time, my lady. He has much to teach us."   *The Marquis' Secret, pp. 178–179*

74

O Lord, I know that the way of man is not
in himself: it is not in man that walketh to
direct his steps.
Jeremiah 10:23

The meek are those who do not assert themselves,
do not defend themselves, never dream of return-
ing anything but good for evil. They do not imagine it their business to take care of themselves.
Self is no umpire in their affairs. . . .

The meek man's self always vanishes in the
light of a real presence. . . . No bristling importance, no vain attendance of fancied rights and
wrongs guards his door or crowds the passages of
his house; they are for angels to come and go.

Knowing the Heart of God, pp. 193–194;
The Hope of the Gospel—"The Heirs of Heaven and Earth"

CREATION *thou dost work by faint degrees,*
By shade and shadow from unseen beginning;
Far, far apart, in unthought mysteries
Of thy own dark, unfathomable seas,
Thou will'st thy will; and thence, upon the earth—
Slow travelling, his way through centuries winning—
A child at length arrives at never ending birth.

WELL *mayst thou then work on indocile hearts*
By small successes, disappointments small;
By nature, weather, failure, or sore fall;
By shame, anxiety, bitterness, and smarts;
By loneliness, by weary loss of zest:
The rags, the husks, the swine, the hunger-quest,
Drive home the wanderer to the Father's breast!

Diary of an Old Soul, July 10, 11

ERROR AND TRUTH

MR. GRAHAM HAD FOR MANY YEARS BEEN more than content to give himself to the hopeful task of training children for the true ends of life.

He would never contradict anything but would oppose error only by teaching truth. He presented truth and set it face to face with error in the minds of his students, leaving the two sides and the growing intellect, heart, and conscience to fight the matter out. To him the business of the teacher was to rouse and urge this battle by leading fresh forces of truth onto the field.

The Fisherman's Lady, p. 39

We are of God: he that knoweth God heareth
us; he that is not of God heareth not us.
Hereby know we the spirit of truth, and the
spirit of error.
1 John 4:6

No teacher should strive to make others think as he thinks, but to lead them to the living Truth, to the Master himself, of whom alone they can learn anything, who will make them in themselves know what is true by the very seeing of it. The inspiration of the Almighty alone gives understanding. To be the disciple of Christ is the end of being, and to persuade others to be his disciples is the aim of all teaching. *Discovering the Character of God, p. 270;*
Unspoken Sermons, Third Series—"Justice"

WAIT AND SEE WHAT GOD WILL DO

RICHARD BEGAN TO WONDER WHETHER EVEN an all-mighty and all-good God could have contrived a world that nobody in it would ever complain of anything. What if he had plans too large for the vision of men to take in, and they would not trust him for what they could not see? Why should not a man at least wait and see what God was going to do with him, perhaps for him, before he accused or denied him? At worst, he would be no worse for the waiting!

What if there was a way so much higher than ours as to include all the seeming right and seeming wrong in one radiance of righteousness? The idea was hardly conceivable! But he would try to hold by it. What we rightfully conceive bad must be bad to God as well as to us; but may there not be things so far above us that we cannot take them in, that seem bad because they are so far above us in goodness that we see them only partially and untruly?

He would try to trust! He would say, "If you are my Father, be my Father, and comfort your child! Perhaps things are not as you would have them, and you are doing what can be done to set them right. Give me time to trust you. Explain the things I am unable to understand."

The Baron's Apprenticeship, pp. 166–167

*For as the heavens are higher than the earth,
so are my ways higher than your ways, and
my thoughts than your thoughts.*
Isaiah 55:9

FINDING TRUTH

TO GIBBIE, BARELEGGED, BAREFOOTED, almost barebodied as he was, sun or shadow made small difference except as one of the musical intervals of the life that make the melody of existence. Hardy through hardship, he knew nothing better than a constant good-humored sparring with nature and circumstances for the privilege of being, enjoyed what came to him thoroughly, never mourned over what he had not, and, like the animals, was at peace.

He had not had much to eat. Half a cookie which a stormy child had thrown away to ease his temper, and a small yellow turnip the green-grocer's wife had given him.

It had been one of his meager days. But it is wonderful upon how little those rare natures capable of making the most of things will live and thrive. There is a great deal more to be gotten out of things than is generally gotten out of them, whether the thing be a chapter of the Bible or a yellow turnip.   *The Baronet's Song, pp. 15–16*

And ye shall eat in plenty, and be satisfied,
and praise the name of the Lord your God,
that hath dealt wondrously with you: and
my people shall never be ashamed.
Joel 2:26

To trust in the strength of God in our weakness—this is the victory that overcomes the world. To believe in God our strength in the face of all seeming denial; to believe in him out of the heart of

weakness and unbelief, in spite of numbness and weariness and lethargy; to believe in the wide-awake reality of his being, through all the stupefying, enervating, distorting dream; to will to wake, when the very being seems athirst for a godless repose—these are the broken steps up to the high fields where repose is but a form of strength, strength but a form of joy, joy but a form of love.

"I am weak," says the true soul, "but not so weak that I would not be strong, not so sleepy that I would not see the sun rise, not so lame but that I would walk! I am weak, but God is strong! Thanks be to him who perfects strength in weakness and gives to his beloved of his very life even while they sleep!"

Discovering the Character of God, p. 22;
Unspoken Sermons, Second Series—"Life"

TO JUNE.
AH, truant, thou art here again, I see!
For in a season of such wretched weather
I thought that thou hadst left us altogether,
Although I could not choose but fancy thee
Skulking about the hill-tops, whence the glee
Of thy blue laughter peeped at times, or rather
Thy bashful awkwardness, as doubtful whether
Thou shouldst be seen in such a company
Of ugly runaways, unshapely heaps
Of ruffian vapour, broken from restraint
Of their slim prison in the ocean deeps.
But yet I may not chide: fall to thy books—
Fall to immediately without complaint—
There they are lying, hills and vales and brooks.

THE PROPER RESPONSE TO MEANNESS

DAWTIE'S FATHER HAD A RARE KEEN instinct for what is mean—not in others, but in himself—and when he saw meanness rear its head, he was abhorred by it. To shades and nuances of selfishness, which men of high repute and comfortable conscience would neither be surprised to find in their neighbors nor annoyed to find in themselves, he would give no quarter. Along with Andrew's father, in childhood and youth Dawtie's father had been under the influence of a simple-hearted pastor, whom the wise and prudent laughed at as one who could not take care of himself. These scoffers were incapable of seeing that, like his Master, the pastor laid down his life that he might take it again. He left God to look after him that he might be free to look after God.

Little Dawtie had learned her catechism, but, thank God, had never thought about it or attempted to understand it—good negative preparation for becoming, in a few years more, able to understand the New Testament with the heart of a babe. *The Landlady's Master, p. 55*

But Jesus said, Suffer little children, and
forbid them not, to come unto me: for of such
is the kingdom of heaven.
Matthew 19:14

WE MUST MAKE GOOD TEMPER OURS

AS AMY LOVINGLY BRUSHED HESTER'S LONG waves, Hester tried to help her understand that she must not think of a happy disposition merely as something that could be put into her and taken out of her. She tried to make her see that everyone has a large supply of good temper at hand, but that to make it truly theirs they must choose it and will to be good-tempered by holding it fast with the hand of determination when the hand of wrong would snatch it away.

"Because I have a book on my shelves," she explained, "does not make it mine. When I have read and understood it, then it is a little mine; when I love it and do what it tells me, then it is altogether mine. It is like that with good temper: if you have it sometimes and not at others, then it is not yours. It lies in you like that book on my table—a thing priceless if it were your own, but as it is, a thing you can't even keep against your poor, weak old aunts." *The Gentlewoman's Choice, pp. 41–42*

Giving all diligence, add to your faith virtue; and to virtue knowledge; and to knowledge temperance; and to temperance patience; and to patience godliness; and to godliness brotherly kindness; and to brotherly kindness charity. For if these things be in you, and abound, they make you that ye shall neither be barren nor unfruitful in the knowledge of our Lord Jesus Christ.

2 Peter 1:5–8

THE MEEK INHERIT

NOT FOR YEARS AND YEARS HAD JANET BEEN to church. She had long been unable to walk so far; and having no book but the best, and no help to understand it but the highest, her faith was simple, strong, real, all-pervading. Day by day she pored over the great gospel until she had grown to be one of the noble ladies of the kingdom of heaven—one of those who inherit the earth and are ripening to see God.

For the Master, and his mind in hers, was her teacher. She had little or no theology save what he taught her. To Janet, Jesus Christ was no object of so-called theological speculation, but a living Man who somehow or other heard her when she called to him, and sent her the help she needed. *The Baronet's Song, p. 44*

The meek will he guide in judgment: and the meek will he teach his way.
Psalms 25:9

We cannot see the world as God means it, except in proportion as our souls are meek.

Only in meekness are we the world's inheritors. Meekness alone makes the spiritual retina pure to receive God's things as they are, mingling with them neither imperfection nor impurity of its own.

A thing so beheld that it conveys to me the divine thought inherent in its very form, that thing is truly mine. Nothing can be mine in any way but through its mediation between God and my life.

In the soul of the meek, the earth remains an endless possession—his because God, who made it, is his. He has the earth by his divine relation to him who sent it forth from him as a tree sends out its leaves. To inherit the earth is to grow ever more alive to the presence, in it and in all its parts, of him who is the life of men.

The man who refuses to assert himself, seeking no recognition by men, leaving the care of his life to the Father, and occupying himself with the will of the Father, shall find himself, by and by, at home in his Father's house, with all the Father's property his.
Knowing the Heart of God, pp. 195–196;
The Hope of the Gospel—"The Heirs of Heaven and Earth"

TOO eager I must not be to understand.
How should the work the Master goes about
Fit the vague sketch my compasses have planned?
I am his house—for him to go in and out.
He builds me now—and if I cannot see
At any time what he is doing with me,
'Tis that he makes the house for me too grand.

The house is not for me—it is for him.
His royal thoughts require many a stair,
Many a tower, many an outlook fair,
Of which I have no thought, and need no care.
Where I am most perplexed, it may be there
Thou mak'st a secret chamber, holy-dim,
Where thou wilt come to help my deepest prayer.
Diary of an Old Soul, July 15, 16

WHO ARE YOU?

"ARE YOU A SOCIETY, THEN?" I ASKED.

"No. At least we don't use the word. And certainly no other society would acknowledge us."

"What are you, then?"

"Why should we be anything, so long as we do our work?"

"Do you lay claim to no designation of any sort?"

"We are a church if you like. There!"

"Who is your clergyman?"

"Nobody."

"Where do you meet?"

"Nowhere."

"What are your rules, then?"

"We have none."

"What makes you a church?"

"Divine service."

"What do you mean by that?"

"The sort of thing you have seen me involved in tonight."

"What is your creed?"

"Jesus Christ."

"But what do you believe about him?"

"We believe *in* him. We consider any belief *in* him—however small—far better than any amount of belief about him."   *The Musician's Quest, p. 218*

> *Then said they unto him, Where is thy*
> *Father? Jesus answered, Ye neither know me,*
> *nor my Father: if ye had known me, ye*
> *should have known my Father also.*
> *John 8:19*

84

THE TROUBLESOME CONDITION OF PRIDE

TO HIS BROTHER, IAN SEEMED HARDLY touched with earthly stain. But despite his large and dominant humanity, Alister was still in the troublesome condition of one trying to do right against a powerful fermentation of pride. He held noblest principles; but the sediment of generations was too easily stirred up to cloud them. He loved his neighbor, but his neighbor was mostly of his own family or his own clan. He *might* have been unjust for the sake of his own—a small fault in the eyes of the world, but a great fault indeed in a nature like his, capable of being so much beyond it. For while the faults of a good man cannot be as evil as the faults of a bad man, they are more blameworthy, and greater faults than the same would be in a bad man.

The Highlander's Last Song, p. 52

The Lord will destroy the house of the proud.
Proverbs 15:25

Jesus tells us we must leave the self altogether—yield it, deny it, refuse it, lose it. Thus *only* shall we save it. . . . The self is given us that we may sacrifice it. It is ours in order that we, like Christ, may have something to offer—not that we should torment it, but that we should deny it; not that we should cross it, but that we should abandon it utterly.

Knowing the Heart of God, p. 117;
Unspoken Sermons, Second Series—"Self Denial"

HAVE I DONE ANYTHING BECAUSE HE SAID DO IT?

"IN MY ROOM, THREE DAYS AGO," THE curate went on, "I was reading the strange story of the man who appeared in Palestine saying that he was the Son of God. And I came upon those words of his which I have just read to you. All at once my conscience awoke and asked me, 'Do you do the things he says to you?' And I thought to myself, 'Have I today done a single thing he has said to me? When was the last time I did something I heard from him? Did I *ever* in all my life do one thing because he said to me, "Do this?"' And the answer was, 'No, never.' Yet there I was, not only calling myself a Christian, but presuming to live among you and be your helper on the road toward the heavenly kingdom. What a living lie I have been!"

"Having made this confession," Wingfold proceeded, "you will understand that whatever I now say, I say to myself as much as to any among you to whom it may apply."

He then showed that faith and obedience are one and the same spirit: what in the heart we call faith, in the will we call obedience. He showed that the Lord refused the faith which found its vent at the lips in worshipping words and not at the limbs in obedient action.

Some of his listeners immediately pronounced his notions bad theology, while others said to themselves that at least it was common sense.

The Curate's Awakening, p. 83

Therefore whosoever heareth these sayings of
mine, and doeth them, I will liken him unto a
wise man, which built his house upon a rock.
Matthew 7:24

Instead of asking yourself whether you believe or not, ask yourself whether you have this day done one single thing because he said, "Do it," or once abstained because he said, "Do not do it." I do not say that you will not have, as a matter of course, done this or that good thing that fell into harmony with the words of Jesus. But have you done or not done any act, as a conscious decision made *because* he said to do it or not?

It is simply absurd to say you believe, or even want to believe in him, if you do not do anything he tells you. You can at once begin to be a disciple of the Living One—by obeying him in the first thing you can think of in which you are not obeying him.   *Knowing the Heart of God, pp. 30–31;*

Unspoken Sermons, Second Series—"The Truth in Jesus"

O MASTER, my desires to work, to know,
To be aware that I do live and grow—
All restless wish for anything not thee,
I yield, and on thy altar offer me.
Let me no more from out thy presence go,
But keep me waiting watchful for thy will—
Even while I do it, waiting watchful still.

Diary of an Old Soul, July 29

DOUBT MAY INDICATE
A LARGER FAITH

IAN WAS ONE OF THOSE BLESSED FEW WHO doubt many things by virtue of a larger faith—causing consternation among those of smaller faith who wrongly see such doubts as signs of unbelief. But while his roots were seeking a deeper soil, his faith could not show so fast a growth above ground. He doubted most about the things he loved best, while he devoted the energies of a mind whose keenness almost masked its power, to discover possible ways of believing them.

To the wise his doubts would have been his best credentials; they were worth ten times the faith of most. It was truth, and higher truth, he was always seeking. The sadness which colored his deepest individuality could be removed only by the conscious presence of the Eternal.   *The Highlander's Last Song, pp. 53–54*

And straightway the father of the child cried
out, and said with tears, Lord, I believe; help
thou mine unbelief.
Mark 9:24

How God can bring about righteousness in you, or me, I cannot tell. Let him do it, and perhaps you will know.   *Discovering the Character of God, p. 178;*
Unspoken Sermons, Third Series—"Righteousness"

TWO ADVANTAGES— TO BE POOR AND TO FEAR GOD

IT MAY SEEM STRANGE THAT THERE SHOULD be three such children together. But their fathers and mothers had for generations been poor—which was a great advantage, as may be seen in the world by him who has eyes to see, and heard in the parable of the rich man by him who has ears to hear.

Also they were God-fearing, which was a far greater advantage and made them honorable. For they would have scorned things that most Christians think nothing of doing. *The Landlady's Master, pp. 54–55*

Then said Jesus unto his disciples, Verily I say unto you, That a rich man shall hardly enter into the kingdom of heaven.
Matthew 19:23

Possessions are *things*. And *things* in general are very apt to prove hostile to the better life. No man can be perfect until, deprived of every*thing*, he can remain calm and content, aware of a well-being untouched; for in no other way would he be possessor of all things, the child of the Eternal.

Knowing the Heart of God, p. 201;
Unspoken Sermons, Second Series—"The Hardness of the Way"

HOW JESUS LOVED WOMEN

ON CERTAIN DAYS WINGFOLD FOUND THAT nothing calmed and brightened Leopold like talking about Jesus. He would begin thinking aloud on some part of the gospel story, that which was most in his mind at the time.

Occasionally he looked up and found his pupil fast asleep—sometimes with a smile, sometimes with a tear on his face. The sight would satisfy him well. Calm upon such a tormented sea must be the gift of God. And the curate would sometimes fall asleep himself—to start awake at the first far-off sound of Helen's dress sweeping over the grass toward them.

One day she came up behind them as they talked. Since the grass had been mown that morning, and also since she happened to be dressed in her riding habit and had gathered up the skirt over her arm, on this occasion she made no sound of sweep approach. Wingfold had been in one of his rambling monologues, and he and Leopold were talking about the women Jesus had spoken to. They discussed the women in the seventh chapter of John—Mary his mother, Mary Magdalene, and the Gentile from Syrophoenicia. Their talk went on a long time, and all the while Helen listened entranced as the curate told Leopold how one could see how much Jesus loved women by the way he talked to them.

Then at the end he said: "How any woman can help casting herself heart and soul at the feet of such a man, I cannot imagine. You do not once read of a woman being against him—except his own mother when she thought he was going astray and forgetting his high mission. The

divine love in him toward his Father in heaven and his brethren was ever melting down his conscious individuality in sweetest showers upon individual hearts. He came down like rain upon the mown grass, like showers that water the earth. No woman, no man surely ever saw him as he was and did not worship him!"

Helen turned and glided silently back into the house, and neither knew she had been there.

The Curate's Awakening, pp. 185–186

*Now when Jesus was in Bethany, in the
house of Simon the leper, there came unto him
a woman having an alabaster box of very
precious ointment, and poured it on his head,
as he sat at meat.*
Matthew 26:6–7

Human science will never discover God. For human science is but the backward undoing of the tapestry-web of God's science, it works with its back to him, and is always leaving him—his intent, that is, his perfected work—behind it, always going farther and farther away from the point where his work culminates in revelation. Doubtless it thus makes some small intellectual approach to him, but at best it can only come to his back. Science will never find the face of God; while those who would reach his heart will find also the spring-head of his science.

*Discovering the Character of God, p. 60;
Unspoken Sermons, Third Series—"The Truth"*

THE DEEPEST CRY OF THE HEART

THE CRY OF THE HUMAN HEART IN ALL AGES is, "Where is God and how shall I know him?"

I know multitudes are incapable of knowing that this is their heart's cry. But if you are one of these, I would ask if you have ever yet made one discovery in your heart. To him who has been making discoveries in it for fifty years, the depths of his heart are yet a mystery. The roots of your heart go down beyond your knowledge—whole eternities beyond it—into the heart of God.

I repeat, whether you know it or not, your heart in its depths is ever crying out for God. Where the man does not know it, it is because the unfaithful self, a would-be monarch, has usurped the consciousness—the carnal man, almost the demon-man, is uppermost, not the Christ-man. If ever the true cry of the heart reaches that self, it calls it childish, and tries to trample it out. That demon-self does not know that a child crying to God is mightier than a warrior armed with steel.

If there was nothing but fine weather in our soul, the carnal self would be too much for the divine self, and would always control it. But bad weather, misfortune, adversity, or whatever name men may call it, sides with the Christ-self deep inside, and helps to make its voice heard.   *The Gentlewoman's Choice, pp. 27–28*

*And call upon me in the day of trouble: I will
deliver thee, and thou shalt glorify me.*
Psalms 50:15

CAN THE
YOUNG OBEY?

MOST OF MY READERS WILL FIND IT HARD
to believe that there should be three persons such as
Andrew, Sandy, and Dawtie, so related, who agreed to
ask of God neither riches nor love, but that he should
take his own way with them, that the Father should work
his will in them, and that he would teach them what he
wanted of them, and help them to do it.

The church is God's elect, and yet you cannot
believe in three holy children? Do you say, "Because they
are represented as beginning to obey so young"?

"But if the young cannot obey," I answer, "then there
can be no principle such as Jesus spoke of, but only an
occasional and arbitrary exercise of spiritual power—in
the perfecting of praise out of the mouth of babes and
sucklings, or in the preference of them to the wise and
prudent as the recipients of divine revelation. If he said
it, I would further contend that what he spoke must be
a principle of truth, not a mere spiritual accident."

The Landlady's Master, p. 76

*And when the chief priests and scribes
saw . . . the children crying in the temple, and
saying, Hosanna to the Son of David; they
were sore displeased, And said unto him,
Hearest thou what these say? And Jesus saith
unto them, Yea; have ye never read, Out of
the mouth of babes and sucklings thou hast
perfected praise?*
Matthew 21:15–16

QUALIFICATIONS FOR THE MINISTRY

"PLEASE BE SEATED," SAID MRS. RAMSHORN, without looking up from her knitting—the seat she offered being the wide meadow.

But they had already done so, and presently were deep in a gentle talk. At length certain words that had been foolhardy enough to wander within her range attracted the notice of Mrs. Ramshorn, and she began to listen. But she could not hear distinctly. She fancied, from certain obscure associations in her own mind, that they were speaking against persons of low origin, who might wish to enter the church for the sake of *bettering themselves*. Holding as she did that no church position should be obtained except by persons of good family and position, she was gratified to hear, as she supposed, the same sentiments from the mouth of such an illiterate person as she imagined Polwarth to be. Therefore, she proceeded to patronize him a little.

"I quite agree with you," she announced. "None but such as you describe should presume to set foot within the sacred precincts of the profession."

"Yes," he agreed, "the great evil in the church has always been the presence in it of persons unsuited for the work required of them there. One very simple sifting rule would be, that no one should be admitted to the clergy who had not first proved himself capable of making a better living in some other calling."

"I cannot go with you so far as that—so few careers are open to gentlemen," rejoined Mrs. Ramshorn. "But it would not be a bad rule that everyone, for admission to holy orders, should possess property sufficient at least

to live on. With that for a foundation, he would occupy the superior position every clergyman ought to have."

"I was thinking," responded Polwarth, "mainly of the experience in life he would gather by having to make his own living. Behind the counter or the plough, or in the workshop, he would come to know men and their struggles and their thoughts."

"Good heavens!" exclaimed Mrs. Ramshorn. "But it is not possible that you can be speaking of the *church*—of the clerical profession."

"I would have no one ordained till after forty," returned Polwarth. "By that time he would know whether he had any real call or only a temptation to the church from the hope of an easy living."

By this time Mrs. Ramshorn had heard more than enough.

"Mr.—Mr.—I don't know your name—you will oblige me by uttering no more such slanders in my company. I am astonished, Mr. Wingfold, at your allowing a member of your congregation to speak with so little regard for the feelings of the clergy. You forget, sir, who said the laborer was worthy of his hire."

"I hope not, madam," responded Polwarth. "I only suggest that though the laborer is worthy of his hire, not every man is worthy of the labor."

The Curate's Awakening, pp. 189–190

*Let the elders that rule well be counted worthy
of double honour, especially they who labour
in the word and doctrine. For the scripture
saith, Thou shalt not muzzle the ox that
treadeth out the corn. And, the labourer is
worthy of his reward.*
1 *Timothy* 5:17–18

WHEN JOB SAW GOD, ALL WAS WELL

IN THE EVENING HE TOOK UP A LEARNED commentary on the Book of Job. But he never even approached the discovery of what Job wanted, received, and was satisfied with in the end. He never saw that what he himself needed, but did not desire, was the same thing—a sight of God! He never discovered that, when God came to Job, Job forgot all he had intended to say to him—did not ask him a single question—because he suddenly knew that all was well.

The student of Scripture remained blind to the fact that the very presence of the Loving One, the Father of men, proved sufficient in itself to answer every question, to still every doubt.

But then James's heart was not pure like Job's, and therefore he could never have seen God. He did not even desire to see him, and so could see nothing as it was. He read with the blindness of the devil of self in his heart. *The Minister's Restoration, p. 94*

Then Job answered the Lord, and said, I have heard of thee by the hearing of the ear: but now mine eye seeth thee. Wherefore I abhor myself, and repent in dust and ashes.

Job 42:1, 5—6

THEY WOULD KNOW BETTER IF THEY WANTED TO

"I AM SO TRIED BY THE THINGS SAID ABOUT God," said Andrew, "by people who think they are pleasing him to speak so. I understand God's patience with the wicked, but I do wonder how he can be so patient with the pious!"

"They don't know better."

"They *would* know better if they wanted to! How are they to know better while they are so sure about everything? I would infinitely rather believe in no God at all than in such a God as they would have me believe in!"

The Landlady's Master, p. 198

He that loveth not knoweth not God;
for God is love.
1 John 4:8

I do not say we are called upon to dispute and defend the truth with logic and argument, but we are called upon to show by our lives that we stand on the side of the truth. But when I say *truth*, I do not mean *opinion*. To treat opinion as if that were truth is grievously to wrong the truth. The soul that loves the truth and tries to be true will know when to speak and when to be silent.

Discovering the Character of God, p. 52;
Unspoken Sermons, Third Series—"Kingship"

DOING THE TRUTH IS LIFE ESSENTIAL

TO DOROTHY'S SURPRISE SHE FOUND THAT since her father's death, many of her doubts began to vanish. She had been lifted into a region higher than those questions which had so disturbed her peace before. From a point of clearer vision she saw things so differently that the questions she had had were no longer relevant. The truth was being lived out in her that the business of life is to live, not to answer every objection that the mind can raise concerning things spiritual. She had *done* that which was given her to do; therefore she progressed up the stairway of life.

It is no matter that a man or woman be unable to explain or understand this or that. It does not matter as long as when they see a truth they do it; to see and not do would at once place them in eternal danger. There is in the man or woman who does the truth, the radiance of life essential—a glory infinitely beyond any that can belong to the intellect. *The Lady's Confession, pp. 229–230*

Choose life, that both thou and thy seed may live: That thou mayest love the Lord thy God, and that thou mayest obey his voice, and that thou mayest cleave unto him: for he is thy life, and the length of thy days.
Deuteronomy 30:19–20

We are not and cannot become true sons and daughters without our will willing his will, our

doing following his making. It was the will of Jesus to be the thing God willed and meant him. He was not the Son of God because he could not help it, but because he willed to be in himself the Son that he was in the divine idea.

So with us: we must *be* the sons we are. We must be sons and daughters in our will. And we can be sons and daughters, saved into the bliss of our being, only by choosing God for the Father he is, and doing his will—yielding ourselves true sons and daughters to the absolute Father.

Therein lies human bliss.

Discovering the Character of God, pp. 91–92;
Unspoken Sermons, Second Series—"Life"

THEY will not, therefore cannot, do not know him.
Nothing they could know, could be God. In sooth,
Unto the true alone exists the truth.
They say well, saying nature doth not show him:
Truly she shows not what she cannot show;
And they deny the thing they cannot know.
Who sees a glory, towards it will go.

Diary of an Old Soul, June 12

WE CANNOT LIVE
BY OURSELVES

WALTER WAS TOO ENAMORED WITH THE idea of becoming great to give heed to becoming true.

When a man is hopeful, he feels strong and can work. The thoughts come and the pen runs. Were he always at his best, what might not a man do! Even the least of men, when they are at their best, can accomplish wonderful things.

But not many can determine their moods. And none—be they poets or economists, teachers or novelists, or businessmen—can guarantee they will always have an energetic and fertile condition of mind any more than they can create their minds in the first place. When the mood changes and hope departs, and the inward atmosphere grows damp and dismal, there may be some whose imagination and energy will yet respond to their call. But yet if some certain kind of illness come, eventually every man must lose his power—both physical and mental.

He is compelled to discover that we did not create ourselves; neither do we live by ourselves.

The Poet's Homecoming, pp. 37–38

*I can of mine own self do nothing: as I hear, I
judge: and my judgment is just; because I seek
not mine own will, but the will of the Father
which hath sent me.*

John 5:30

100

Dreams Truly Dreamed

Up and down the little garden Cosmo walked, revolving many things in his mind. "What is this world and its ways," he said, "but a dream that dreams itself out and is gone!"

The majority of men worship solidity and fact. But even a face may be a mere shread for the winds of the limbo of vanities. Everything that *can* pass away—however solid it may temporarily be—belongs to the same category with the dream. The question is whether the passing body leaves a live soul; whether the dream has been truly dreamed, the life lived aright. For there is a reality beyond all facts of suns and systems, wealth and lands, houses and possessions. Solidity itself is but the shadow of a divine necessity, and there may be more truth in a parable than in a whole biography.

Where life and truth are one, there is no passing, no dreaming more. To that waking all dreams truly dreamed are guiding the dreamer. *The Laird's Inheritance, p. 332*

> *He . . . spake a parable, because . . . they*
> *thought that the kingdom of God should*
> *immediately appear.*
> Luke 19:11

The highest condition of the human will is when, not seeing God, it yet holds him fast.

Knowing the Heart of God, p. 302;
Unspoken Sermons, First Series—"The Eloi"

WHO CAN SAY WHAT THE LORD CAN'T DO?

"MAYBE THE BONNY MAN, AS STEENIE CALLS him," said David, "has as much compassion for the poor thing in his heart as Steenie himself."

"Oh, ay! But what can the bonny man himself do, now that's she's dead?"

"Don't limit the Almighty, woman. The Lord of mercy'll manage to look after the little lamb he made, one way or another, there as here. You dare not say he didn't do his best for her here, and will he not do his best for her there as well?"

"Doubtless, David! But you frighten me! It sounds just like papistry to talk about God doing something for her after she's so dead. What *can* he do? He can't die again for the one that wouldn't turn to him in this life. The thing's not to be thought of!"

"How do you know that? You have just thought it yourself. If I was you, I wouldn't dare to say what the Lord couldn't do! There's too many folks already doing that, saying the Lord's atonement can't go beyond what they can't see with their own earth-bound eyes. We can't know Phemy's heart, now, can we? In the meantime, what he makes me able to hope, I'm not going to fling from me!"

David was a true man. He could not believe a thing with one half of his mind and care nothing about it with the other. He, like his Steenie, believed in the bonny man about in the world, not in the mere image of him standing in the precious shrine of the New Testament. The Gospels were to him *life*, not mere past history to

be read and analyzed and placed on his mental shelf of
inactivity. *The Peasant Girl's Dream, pp. 157–158*

*For the bread of God is he which cometh
down from heaven, and giveth life unto the
world.*
John 6:33

A fact, which in itself is of no value, becomes at
once a matter of moral life and death when a man
has the imperative choice of being true or false
concerning it. When the truth, the heart, the summit, the crown of a thing is perceived by a man, he
approaches the fountain of truth whence the thing
came, and perceiving God by understanding what
it is, becomes more of a man, more of the being he
was meant to be. In virtue of this perceived truth,
he has relations with the universe until then undeveloped in him. But far higher will the doing of
the least, the most insignificant duty raise him.

There, in the obedience of his *actions*, he begins
to be a true man. *Discovering the Character of God, p. 66;
Unspoken Sermons, Third Series—"The Truth"*

IN THE WILL
IS STRENGTH

MOLLY STOOD WHERE SHE WAS FOR another moment or two, and Walter gazed up at her till his eyes were wearied with the brightness she reflected and his heart made strong by the better brightness she radiated. For Molly was the very type of a creature born of the sun and ripened by his light and heat—a glowing fruit of the tree of life amid its healing foliage, all splendor and color and overflowing strength.

Self-will is weakness. The will to do right is strength. Molly had made a lifelong habit of willing the right thing and holding to it. Hence it was that she was so gentle. She walked lightly over the carpet, because she could run up a hill like a hare. When she caught selfishness in her, she was down upon it to crush it with the knee and grasp of a giant. Strong indeed is the man or woman whose eternal life subjects the individual "liking" to the perfect will. Such man, such woman, is a free man or free woman indeed! *The Poet's Homecoming, p. 164*

And be not conformed to this world: but be ye
transformed by the renewing of your mind,
that ye may prove what is that good, and
acceptable, and perfect, will of God.
Romans 12:2

THE FIRST DUTY OF MARRIED PEOPLE

"WHAT DO YOU THINK THE FIRST DUTY OF married people, Mercy—to each other, I mean?" said the chief.

"To always be what they look," answered Mercy.

"Yes, but I mean actively. What is their first duty to do toward each other?"

"I can't answer that without thinking."

"Isn't it to help the other to do the will of God?"

"I would say *yes* if I were sure I really meant it."

"You will mean it one day."

"Are you sure God will teach me?"

"I think he wants to do that more than anything else."

"More than to save us?"

"What is saving but taking us out of the dark into the light? There is no salvation but to know God and grow like him." *The Highlander's Last Song, pp. 208–209*

For God, who commanded the light to shine
out of darkness, hath shined in our hearts, to
give the light of the knowledge of the glory of
God in the face of Jesus Christ.
2 Corinthians 4:6

CAN WE TRUST MAJORITY OPINION?

THE OLD LAIRD HAD A NOTEWORTHY MENTAL fabric. Believing himself a true lover of literature, especially of poetry, he would lecture for ten minutes on the right mode of reading a verse in Milton or Dante, but as to meaning would pin his faith to the majority of the commentators. He was discriminative to a degree altogether admirable as to the rightness or wrongness of a proposition with regard to conduct, never questioning within his soul whether there was any injunction upon himself to live by said propositions.

He was almost as orthodox as Paul before his conversion, lacking only the heart and courage to persecute. Whatever the eternal wisdom he saw in him, the thing most present to his own consciousness was the love of rare historic relics. And this love was so mingled in warp and woof that he did not know whether a thing was more precious to him for its rarity, its monetary value, or its historic-reliquary interest.

It hardly yet occurred to him that he must one day leave his things and exist without them, no longer to brood over them, take them in his hands, turn, and stroke, and admire them. Yet, strange to say, he would at times anxious seek to satisfy himself that he was safe for a better world, as he *called* it—to feel certain, that is, that his faith was of the sort he supposed intended by Paul. Not that he himself had actually gathered anything from the writings of the apostle. All his notion came from the traditions of his church concerning the teaching of the apostle.   *The Landlady's Master, pp. 98–99*

Now when Jesus heard these things, he said
unto him, Yet lackest thou one thing: sell all
that thou hast, and distribute unto the poor,
and thou shalt have treasure in heaven: and
come, follow me. And when he heard this, he
was very sorrowful: for he was very rich.
And when Jesus saw that he was very
sorrowful, he said, How hardly shall they
that have riches enter into the kingdom of God!
Luke 18:22–24

What is faith in Christ?

It is the leaving of your way, your objects, your self, and the taking of his and him; the leaving of your trust in men, in money, in opinion, in character, in religious doctrines and opinions, *and then doing as Christ tells you.*

I can find no words strong enough to serve for the weight of this necessity—this obedience.

It is the one terrible heresy of the church that it has always been presenting something else than obedience as faith in Christ.

Knowing the Heart of God, p. 29;
Unspoken Sermons, Second Series—"The Truth in Jesus"

DO NOT TRY TO SET ALL THINGS RIGHT

"THE SCOUNDREL!" CRIED COSMO. "I SHOULD like to give him a good drubbing!"

"Cosmo, my boy," said his father, "you are meddling with what does not belong to you."

"I know it's your business, father, not mine, but—"

"It's no more my business than yours, my son! *'Vengeance is mine, saith the Lord.'* And the best of it is, he'll take no more than's good for the sinner, whereas yourself, Cosmo, in the mood you're in now, would damn the poor old man forever and ever! Man, he can't hurt me to the worth of such a heap of firing!"

Then changing his tone to absolute seriousness, "Mind too, Cosmo," he went on, "that the Master never threatened, but always left the thing, whatever it was, to him that judges righteously. You want nothing but fair play, my son, and whether you get it from our neighbor Lickmyloof or not, there's One that won't keep it from you. You'll get it, my son, you'll get it! The Master'll have all things set right in the end. And if *he* isn't in a hurry, we may well bide our time too. For myself, the man has smitten me upon the one cheek, and may have the other to do on what he likes. It's not worth lifting my old arm to hold off the smack."

The Laird's Inheritance, pp. 244–245

But I say unto you, That ye resist not evil:
but whosoever shall smite thee on thy right
cheek, turn to him the other also.
Matthew 5:39

NO MAN IS A FOOL WHO DOES HIS WORK

I NEED HARDLY SAY WALTER FOUND HIS first lonely evening back in his London lodgings dull. He was not yet capable of looking beneath the look of anything. He felt cabined, cribbed, confined. His world-clothing came too near him. From the flowing robes of a park, a great house, large rooms, wide staircases—with plenty of air and space, color, softness, fitness, completeness—he found himself in the worn, tight, shabby garment of his cheap London room!

But Walter, far from being a wise man, was not therefore a fool. He was not one whom this world cannot teach. No man is a fool who having work to do sets himself to do it, and this Walter did.

The Poet's Homecoming, p. 91

And let the beauty of the Lord our God be
upon us: and establish thou the work of our
hands upon us; yea, the work of our hands
establish thou it.
Psalms 90:17

Oh the folly of any mind that would explain God before obeying him, that would map out the character of God, instead of crying, "Lord, what wouldst thou have me to do?"

Discovering the Character of God, p. 248;
Unspoken Sermons, Third Series—"Justice"

DOES GOD GIVE WHATEVER WE ASK?

"IS IT TRUE THAT YOU BELIEVE GOD GIVES you whatever you ask?"

"I believe God answers all prayer," replied Andrew, "but the shape of the answer depends largely upon the heart of the person praying. Selfish prayers he must doubtless answer differently than selfless prayers. For myself, I have never asked anything of him that he did not give me."

"Would you mind telling me anything you have asked of him? Do you pray for rain for your crops?"

Andrew laughed. "Such things I do not pray for."

"What do you pray for, then?"

"I have never yet required to ask anything not included in the prayer, 'Thy will be done!'"

"That will be done without your praying for it."

"I do not believe it will be done, to all eternity, in the place where it needs doing the most, without my praying for it."

"Where is that?"

"Where first I am accountable that his will should be done?" he asked. "Is it not in myself, in my own heart? And how is his will to be done in *me* without *my* willing it? Does he not want me to love what he loves? To be like himself? To do his will with the glad effort of my will? In a word, to will what he wills? And when I find I cannot, what am I to do but pray for help? I pray, and he helps me."

"There is nothing so strange in that."

"Surely not. It seems to me the simplest of common sense. It is my business, the business of every man, every

woman, every child, that God's will be done by their obedience to that will the moment they know it."

The Landlady's Master, pp. 141–142

*And he was withdrawn from them about a
stone's cast, and kneeled down, and prayed,
Saying, Father, if thou be willing, remove this
cup from me: nevertheless not my will, but
thine, be done.*
Luke 22:41–42

God is the heritage of the soul of origin. Man is the offspring of his making will, of his very life. God himself is man's birthplace. God is the self that makes the soul able to say, I too, *am*.

This absolute unspeakable bliss of the creature is that for which the Son died, for which the Father suffered with him—to regain the *oneness* of man and God. Then only is life right, is as it should be and was meant to be.

Knowing the Heart of God, p. 47;
Unspoken Sermons, Second Series—"The Truth in Jesus"

TRUE MAKING, TRUE CREATING

THE SO-CALLED *CREATIONS* OF THE HUMAN intellect and of the human imagination are spoken of. But there is nothing man can do that comes half so near the true "making," the true creativity of the Maker, as the ordering of his own way. There is only one thing that is higher . . . and that is to will the will of the Father. That act contains an element of the purely creative, and when man does will such, then he is most like God.

To do what we ought to do, as children of God, is an altogether higher, more divine, more potent, more creative thing than to write the grandest poem, paint the most beautiful picture, carve the mightiest statue, build the most magnificent temple, dream out the most enchanting symphony.   *A Daughter's Devotion, pp. 122–123*

And now, O Father, glorify thou me with
thine own self with the glory which I had
with thee before the world was.
John 17:5

Do not imagine that we can do anything ourselves without God. If we choose the right at last, it is all God's doing, and only the more his that it is ours, only in a far more marvelous way than if he had kept us filled with holy impulses precluding the need of choice.   *Knowing the Heart of God, p. 301;*
Unspoken Sermons, First Series—"The Eloi"

WHAT IS THE TRUTH?

WINGFOLD WAS HIGHLY AMUSED AT THE turn things had taken. Polwarth looked annoyed at having allowed himself to be beguiled into such an utterly useless beating of the air.

"My friend *has* some rather unusual notions," interjected the curate. "But you must admit that it was you who encouraged him to go on."

"My husband used to say that very few of the clergy realized how they were envied by the lower classes. To low human nature the truth has always been unpalatable."

What precisely she meant by "the truth" it would be hard to say, but it was always associated, in her mind at least, with a cathedral choir and a portly person in silk stockings.   *The Curate's Awakening, pp. 189–190*

Then Peter opened his mouth, and said, . . .
God is no respecter of persons.
Acts 10:34

The kingdom of God is the home of perfect brotherhood. The poor, the beggars in spirit, the men of humble heart, the unambitious for selfish gain, the unselfish, those who never despise men and never seek their praises, the lowly who see nothing to admire in themselves and therefore cannot seek to be admired of others, the men who give themselves and what they have away—*these* are the free men of the kingdom, *these* are the citizens of the new Jerusalem.   *Knowing the Heart of God, p. 184;*
        The Hope of the Gospel—"The Heirs of Heaven and Earth"

WHAT THOUGHTS DEMAND OF US

NO ONE WOULD HAVE LOOKED INTO THE refined face of Walter Colman and imagined him cherishing sordid views of life. Asked what of all things he most admired, he might truly answer, "the imaginative intellect." He was a fledgling poet. He worshipped what he called thoughts, and would rave about a thought in the abstract. When a concrete thinkable one fell to him, he was jubilant over the isolated thing. But his joy had nothing to do with its value or any practical result.

Of the *doing* of any action as a necessary result of some thought or idea, Walter never considered the possibility. Thoughts and actions were to him as separate as night and day. That thoughts might *demand* action would have been an idea to him unthinkable. What could the one possibly have to do with the other?

The Poet's Homecoming, p. 24

The Lord knoweth the thoughts of man, that
they are vanity.
Psalms 94:11

I hate vain thoughts: but thy law do I love.
Psalms 119:113

One chief cause of the amount of unbelief in the world is that those who have seen something of the glory of Christ set themselves to theorize con-

cerning him rather than to obey him. In teaching others, they have not taught them Christ, but taught *about* Christ. More eager after credible theory than after doing the truth, they have speculated in a condition of heart in which it was impossible they should understand. They have presumed to explain a Christ whom years and years of obedience could alone have made them able to comprehend.

Discovering the Character of God, p. 250;
Unspoken Sermons, Third Series—"Justice"

I AM a fool when I would stop and think,
And lest I lose my thoughts, from duty shrink.
It is but avarice in another shape.
'Tis as the vine-branch were to hoard the grape,
Nor trust the living root beneath the sod.
What trouble is that child to thee, my God,
Who sips thy gracious cup, and will not drink!

True, faithful action only is the life,
The grapes for which we feel the pruning knife.
Thoughts are but leaves; they fall and feed the ground.
The holy seasons, swift and slow, go round;
The ministering leaves return, fresh, large, and rife—
But fresher, larger, more thoughts to the brain—
Farewell, my dove! Come back, hope-laden, through the rain.

Diary of an Old Soul, August 9, 10

HONOR FOR HONESTY

MAKING THINGS IS HIGHER IN THE SCALE OF reality than any mere transmission, than buying and selling, to whatever godly end that may be done as well. Besides, it is easier to do honest work than to buy and sell honestly. The more honor, of course, to those who are honest under the greater difficulty!

But the man who knows how important is the prayer, "Lead us not into temptation," knows that he must not be tempted into temptation even by the glory of duty under difficulty. In humility we must choose the easiest, as we must hold our faces unflinchingly to the hardest, even to the seeming impossible, when it is given us to do. *A Daughter's Devotion, p. 313*

I exhort therefore, that, first of all,
supplications, prayers, intercessions, and
giving of thanks, be made for all men; For
kings, and for all that are in authority; that
we may lead a quiet and peaceable life in all
godliness and honesty.
1 Timothy 2:1–2

To deny oneself is to act no more from the standing ground of self. . . . No longing after the praise of men influence a single throb of the heart.

Right deeds, and not the judgment thereupon; true words, and not what reception they may have, shall be our concern. *Knowing the Heart of God, p. 118;*
Unspoken Sermons, Second Series—"Self Denial"

THE GOOD NEWS DWELT WITH HIM

MAGGIE LOOKED IN AT THE WINDOW AND got a last sight of her father. The sun was shining into the little bare room, and her shadow fell upon him as she passed. But his form lingered clear in the chamber of her mind after she had left him far behind her. There it was not her shadow, but rather the shadow of a great peace that rested upon him as he bent over the shoe, his mind fixed indeed upon his work, but far more occupied with the affairs of quite another region.

Mind and soul were so absorbed in their accustomed labor that never did either interfere with that of the other. His shoemaking lost nothing when he was deepest sunk in the words of his Lord which he was seeking to understand. In his leisure hours he was an intense reader, but it was nothing in any book that now occupied him; it was instead the live good news, the man Jesus Christ himself. In thought, in love, in imagination, that man dwelt in him, was alive in him, and made him alive.

For the cobbler believed absolutely in the Lord of Life, was always trying to do the things he said, and to keep his words abiding in him. Therefore, he made the best shoes, because the work of the Lord did abide in him.   *The Minister's Restoration, p. 23*

Therefore, my beloved brethren, be ye stedfast,
unmoveable, always abounding in the work
of the Lord, forasmuch as ye know that your
labour is not in vain in the Lord.
1 Corinthians 15:58

THE CALL IS TO CHRISTLIKENESS

HAVING HIMSELF LEARNED THE LESSON that so long as a man is dependent on anything earthly he is not a free man, Ian was very desirous to have his brother free also. Alister was a good man: why, then, are those who are trying to be good more continuously troubled with lessons of conscience than the indifferent? Simply, as a man advances, more and more is required of him. A wrong thing in a good man becomes more and more wrong as he draws nearer to freedom from it. His friends may say how seldom he offends, but every time he does offend, he is the more to blame—as he himself knows better than any other.

The chief was one in whom was no guile, but he was far from perfect: any man is far from perfect whose sense of well-being can be altered by change of circumstance. A man unable to do without this thing or that is not yet in sight of his godly perfection, therefore not yet out of sight of suffering. For it is to the perfection of Christlikeness God calls us, and will bring about in us, no matter how many so-called believers would rather settle for something far less, thinking all God wants from us is that we "be ourselves."

Clouds were gathering to burst in fierce hail on the head of the chief, to the end that he might be set free from yet another of the cords that bound him to the earth. He was like a soaring eagle from whose foot hung, trailing to the earth, the line by which his tyrant could at will pull him back to his inglorious perch.

The Highlander's Last Song, pp. 168–169

*Therefore we are buried with him by baptism
into death: that like as Christ was raised up
from the dead by the glory of the Father, even
so we also should walk in newness of life.*
Romans 6:4

*But as he which hath called you is holy, so
be ye holy in all manner of conversation;
Because it is written, Be ye holy; for I am
holy.*
1 Peter 1:15—16

The justice of God is this, that he gives every man,
woman, child, and beast, everything that has
being, fair play. He renders to every man according
to his work. And therein lies his perfect mercy, for
nothing else could be merciful to the man, and
nothing but mercy could be fair to him.

Discovering the Character of God, p. 248;
Unspoken Sermons, Third Series—"Justice"

A TIME TO DO OR A TIME TO WAIT

"SOMETHING MUST BE DONE," DAWTIE WENT on. "He can't be left like that. But if he has any love for his Master, how is it that the love of the Master does not cast out the love of mammon? I can't understand it!"

"That is a hard question. But a cure may be going on, and for some it takes a long time, even years to work it out."

"What if it shouldn't be begun yet!"

"That would be terrible."

"Then what am I to do, Andrew? You always say we must *do* something. You say there is no faith but that which *does* something."

"The apostle James said so, a few years before I was born, Dawtie."

"Don't make fun of me—please, Andrew."

"Make fun of you, Dawtie! Never! But I don't know how to answer you."

"Well then, what *am* I to do?" persisted Dawtie.

"Wait until you know what to do. When you don't know what to do, don't do anything—and only keep asking the Thinker for wisdom."

The Landlady's Master, p. 96

But let patience have her perfect work, that ye
may be perfect and entire, wanting nothing. If
any of you lack wisdom, let him ask of God,
that giveth to all men liberally, and
upbraideth not; and it shall be given him.

James 1:4–5

God Sees Differences of Which the World Takes No Heed

ONCE MORE OUT IN THE COUNTRY, THE beauties of the world began to work the will of its Maker upon Isy's poor lacerated soul. And afar in its hidden deeps the process of healing was already begun. Hope was lifting a feeble head above the tangled weeds of the subsiding deluge, and before long the girl would be able to see and understand how little the Father, whose judgment in the truth of things, cares what at any time his child may have been or done the moment that child gives herself up to be made what he would have her!

Looking down into the hearts of men, he sees differences there of which the self-important world takes no heed. For indeed, many that count themselves of the first, he sees the last—and what he sees, alone *is*. Kings and emperors may be utterly forgotten, while a gutter-child, a thief, a girl who in this world never had even a notion of purity, may lie smiling in the arms of the Eternal, while the head of a lordly house that still flourishes like a green bay-tree, may be wandering about with the dogs beyond the walls of the city.

The Minister's Restoration, p. 113

But many that are first shall be last;
and the last shall be first.
Matthew 19:30

HE KNOWS WHAT
YOU NEED

"SO YOU COUNT SOCIETIES, THEN, OF NO USE in helping the poor?"

"I avoid all attempt at organization. What I want is simply to be a friend of the poor. I bide my time. I do not preach or set about to institute a program to remove this or that ill from our society. I go where I am led. In fact, I usually wait till I am asked to offer assistance. And even then I often refuse to give the sort of help they want. The worst thing you can do for them is to attempt to save them from the natural consequences of wrong; although you may sometimes help them out of them.

"But it is right to do many things for them when you know them, which would not help if you didn't. I am among them. They know me. Their children know me. Something is always occurring that makes this or that person come to me. In my labor I am content to do the thing that lies next to me. I await events."

"There is no place for me in your work, then?"

"You have had no training to fit you for such a work. Of course there is a place for you, but I could not possibly direct you. To get the training you need, you must simply begin where you are, do the thing that lies next to you, help the next person you encounter. I am sorry I cannot give you more specific direction."

"Yes. That is why I came to you."

"Just so. I cannot give you the sort of help you desire. Go and ask it of the One who can."

"Speak more plainly."

"Well, then, if God is your Father, he will listen to you his child. He will teach you everything."

"But I don't know what I want, even what to ask him to teach me."

"He does. Ask him to tell you what you want. Read the gospels. Read the story of Jesus as if you had never read it before. He was a man who had the secret of life which your heart is longing for."

The Musician's Quest, pp. 227–228

Pure religion and undefiled before God and the Father is this, To visit the fatherless and widows in their affliction, and to keep himself unspotted from the world.

James 1:27

Come to God, then, my brother, my sister, with all your desires and instincts, all your lofty ideals, all your longing for purity and unselfishness, all your yearning to love and be true, all your aspirations after self-forgetfulness and child-life in the breath of the Father. Come to him with all your weaknesses, all your shames, all your futilities; with all your helplessness over your own thoughts; with all your failures, yes, the sick sense of having missed the tide of true affairs. Come to him with all your doubts, fears, dishonesties, meanness, paltriness, misjudgments, weariness, disappointments, and staleness. Be sure he will take you with all your miserable brood into the care of his limitless heart!

Discovering the Character of God, p. 157;
Unspoken Sermons, Third Series—"Light"

A LIVE AND
WATCHING READINESS

IN TRUTH THE COBBLER BELIEVED THAT THE Lord of men was often walking to and fro in the earthly kingdom of his Father, watching what was going on there, and doing his best to bring it to its true and ideal condition.

Never did John MacLear lift his eyes heavenward without a vague feeling that he might that very moment catch a sight of the glory of his coming Lord. If ever he fixed his eyes on the far horizon, it was never without receiving a shadowy suggestion that, like a sail towering over the edge of the world, the first great flag of the Lord's hitherward march might that moment be rising between earth and heaven. For certainly he would come unawares.

Thus, he was ever on the watch. And yet even when deepest lost in such watching for his Savior, the lowest whisper of humanity was always loud enough to recall him to his "live work"—to wake him, that is, to those around him, lest he should be found asleep to the needs of others at the moment of his Lord's coming.

As his daily work was ministration to the weary feet of his Master's men, so was his soul ever awake to their sorrows and spiritual necessities.

The Minister's Restoration, pp. 126–127

Watch therefore, for ye know neither the day
nor the hour wherein the Son of man cometh.
Matthew 25:13

TO ADMIRE DOES NOT MAKE US EQUAL WITH OUR HERO

ALL THE COMMON SENSE WAS ON THE SIDE of the girl, and she had been doing her best to make the boy more practical—hitherto without much success, although he was by no means a bad sort of fellow. He had not yet passed the stage—some appear never to pass it in this world—in which an admirer feels himself in the same category with his hero. Many are content with themselves because they side with those whose ways they do not endeavor to follow.

Such are most who call themselves Christians. If men admired themselves for what they did, their conceit would be greatly moderated.

The Peasant Girl's Dream, p. 15

The rich man is wise in his own conceit; but the poor that hath understanding searcheth him out.
Proverbs 28:11

If you do not do what you know of the truth, I do not wonder that you seek it intellectually. But do not call anything that may be so gained, *the Truth.* . . . Obey the truth, I say, and let theory wait. Theory must spring from life, but never life from theory.

Discovering the Character of God, p. 268;
Unspoken Sermons, Third Series—"Justice"

THE OTHER SIDE OF DEATH

MALCOLM FOUND HIS FRIEND SEATED ON A stone in the churchyard. "See," said the schoolmaster, "how the shadow from one grave stretches like an arm to embrace another. In this light the churchyard seems the very birthplace of shadows." A brief silence followed. "Does the morning or evening light suit such a place best, Malcolm?"

"The evening light, sir," he answered at length, "for you see the sun's like dying, and death's like falling asleep, and the grave's the bed and the sod is the bedclothes, and there's a long night ahead."

"Are you sure of that, Malcolm? Come here," said Mr. Graham. "Read that," he said, pointing to a flat gravestone covered with moss but the inscription nevertheless stood out clearly: "He is not here; he is risen."

Malcolm gazed, trying to think what his master would have him think. Mr. Graham resumed: "If he is risen—if the sun is up, Malcolm—then the morning and not the evening is the season for the place of the tombs; the morning when the shadows are shortening and separating, not the evening when they are growing all into one. I used to love the churchyard best in the evening, when the past was more to me than the future. But now I visit it almost every bright summer morning and only occasionally at night."

"But, sir, isn't death a dreadful thing?" asked Malcolm.

"That depends on whether a man regards it as his fate or as the will of a perfect God. Its obscurity is its dread. But if God be light, then death itself must be full

of splendor—a splendor probably too keen for our eyes to receive." *The Fisherman's Lady, pp. 55–56*

So when this corruptible shall have put on
incorruption, and this mortal shall have put
on immortality, then shall be brought to pass
the saying that is written,
Death is swallowed up in victory.
1 Corinthians 15:54

The truth of every man is the perfected Christ in him. As Christ is the blossom of humanity, so the blossom of every man is the Christ perfected in him. The vital force of humanity working in him is Christ; He is his root—the generator and perfecter of his individuality. The stronger the pure will of the man to be true, the freer and more active his choice, the more definite his individuality, ever the more is the man and all that is his, Christ's. Without him he could not have been; being, he could not have become capable of truth; capable of truth, he could never have loved it; loving and desiring it, he could not have attained to it.

Discovering the Character of God, p. 68;
Unspoken Sermons, Third Series—"The Truth"

BETTER TO DENY GOD THAN REBEL AGAINST HIM

ONCE MORE THE LOUD COMPLAINT against life awoke and raged. What an evil thing life was! Again and again he cried out against God for the misery he had caused. Even if he had not caused it, could he not prevent it? And if he could prevent it, then why did he allow it?

It is surely a notable argument against the existence of God, that they who believe in him believe in him so wretchedly! So many carry themselves to him like peevish children. Richard half believed in God, only to complain of him altogether. Would it not be better to deny him altogether than to murmur and rebel against him?

But perhaps it is better to complain, if one complains to God himself.

Does he not then draw nigh to God with what truth is in him? And will he not then fare as Job, to whom God drew nigh in return, and set his heart at rest?

The Baron's Apprenticeship, p. 166

*I know thy works, that thou art neither cold
nor hot: I would thou wert cold or hot.*
Revelation 3:15